P9-BZI-795

# AMERICAN HUNGER

# AMERICAN HUNGER

## Richard Wright

Afterword by Michel Fabre

*1817*

HARPER & ROW, PUBLISHERS

New York, Hagerstown, San Francisco, London

A portion of this work originally appeared in the *Atlantic Monthly* and *Dissent.*

AMERICAN HUNGER. Copyright 1944 by Richard Wright. Copyright © 1977 by Ellen Wright. Afterword copyright © 1977 by Michel Fabre. All rights reserved. Printed in the United States of America. No part of this book may be used or reproduced in any manner whatsoever without written permission except in the case of brief quotations embodied in critical articles and reviews. For information address Harper & Row, Publishers, Inc., 10 East 53rd Street, New York, N.Y. 10022. Published simultaneously in Canada by Fitzhenry & Whiteside Limited, Toronto.

FIRST EDITION

*Designed by C. Linda Dingler*

Library of Congress Cataloging in Publication Data

Wright, Richard, 1908–1960.
    American hunger.
    Autobiographical.
    Continues Black boy.
    1. Wright, Richard, 1908–1960. 2. Authors, American
—20th century—Biography. I. Title.
PS3545.R815Z498   1977      813'.5'2   [B]      76–47248
ISBN 0–06–014768–7

77 78 79 80 81 10 9 8 7 6 5 4 3 2 1

# Publisher's Note

The book published here was originally included by Richard Wright as the second part of an autobiography entitled *American Hunger.* Its working title was "The Horror and the Glory."

The two parts were separated prior to publication and the first part was published in 1945 as *Black Boy,* the second apparently being intended for publication at a later date. Portions of the second section saw scattered publication in the 1940s, but with this volume it now appears intact for the first time.

# Acknowledgment

The text of *American Hunger* has been printed from the original page proofs of 1944, as corrected by the author. These proofs are now a part of the Richard Wright Archive in the Beinecke Rare Book and Manuscript Library of Yale University.

Harper & Row gratefully acknowledges the cooperation and aid of the Supervisory Committee of the Richard Wright Archive: Charles Davis, Michel Fabre, Donald Gallup, Louis Martz, and Ellen Wright.

Also our thanks to John Sterling of Paul R. Reynolds, Inc., Richard Wright's literary agent.

*Sometimes I wonder, huh,*
*Wonder if other people wonder, huh,*
*Sometimes I wonder, huh,*
*Wonder if other people wonder, huh,*
*Just like I do, oh, my Lord, just like I do!*

—Negro Folk Song

# AMERICAN HUNGER

# Chapter I

M Y first glimpse of the flat black stretches of Chicago depressed and dismayed me, mocked all my fantasies. Chicago seemed an unreal city whose mythical houses were built of slabs of black coal wreathed in palls of gray smoke, houses whose foundations were sinking slowly into the dank prairie. Flashes of steam showed intermittently on the wise horizon, gleaming translucently in the winter sun. The din of the city entered my consciousness, entered to remain for years to come. The year was 1927.

What would happen to me here? Would I survive? My expectations were modest. I wanted only a job. Hunger had long been my daily companion. Diversion and recreation, with the exception of reading, were unknown. In all my life—though surrounded by many people—I had not had a single satisfying, sustained relationship with another human being and, not having had any, I did not miss it. I made no demands whatever upon others.

The train rolled into the depot. Aunt Maggie and I got off and walked slowly through the crowds into the station. I looked about to see if there were signs saying: FOR WHITE—FOR COLORED. I saw none. Black people and white people moved about, each seemingly intent upon his private mission. There was no racial fear. Indeed, each person acted as though no one existed but himself. It was strange to pause before a crowded newsstand and buy a newspaper without having to wait until a white man was

1

served. And yet, because everything was so new, I began to grow tense again, although it was a different sort of tension than I had known before. I knew that this machine-city was governed by strange laws and I wondered if I would ever learn them.

As we waited for a streetcar to take us to Aunt Cleo's home for temporary lodging, I looked northward at towering buildings of steel and stone. There were no curves here, no trees; only angles, lines, squares, bricks and copper wires. Occasionally the ground beneath my feet shook from some faraway pounding and I felt that this world, despite its massiveness, was somehow dangerously fragile. Streetcars screeched past over steel tracks. Cars honked their horns. Clipped speech sounded about me. As I stood in the icy wind, I wanted to talk to Aunt Maggie, to ask her questions, but her tight face made me hold my tongue. I was learning already from the frantic light in her eyes the strain that the city imposed upon its people. I was seized by doubt. Should I have come here? But going back was impossible. I had fled a known terror, and perhaps I could cope with this unknown terror that lay ahead.

The streetcar came. Aunt Maggie motioned for me to get on and pushed me toward a seat in which a white man sat looking blankly out the window. I sat down beside the man and looked straight ahead of me. After a moment I stole a glance at the white man out of the corners of my eyes; he was still staring out the window, his mind fastened upon some inward thought. I did not exist for him; I was as far from his mind as the stone buildings that swept past in the street. It would have been illegal for me to sit beside him in the part of the South that I had come from.

The car swept past soot-blackened buildings, stopping at each block, jerking again into motion. The conductor called street names in a tone that I could not understand. People got on and off the car, but they never glanced at one another. Each person seemed to regard the other as a part of the city landscape. The white man who sat beside me rose and I turned my knees aside to let him pass, and another white man sat beside me and buried his face in a newspaper. How could that possibly be? Was he conscious of my blackness?

We went to Aunt Cleo's address and found that she was living in a rented room. I had imagined that she lived in an apartment and I was disappointed. I rented a room from Aunt Cleo's landlady and decided to keep it until I got a job. I was baffled. Everything seemed makeshift, temporary. I caught an abiding sense of insecurity in the personalities of the people around me. I found Aunt Cleo aged beyond her years. Her husband, a product of a southern plantation, had, like my father, gone off and left her. Why had he left? My aunt could not answer. She was beaten by the life of the city, just as my mother had been beaten. Wherever my eyes turned they saw stricken, frightened black faces trying vainly to cope with a civilization that they did not understand. I felt lonely. I had fled one insecurity and had embraced another.

When I rose the next morning the temperature had dropped below zero. The house was as cold to me as the southern streets had been in winter. I dressed, doubling my clothing. I ate in a restaurant, caught a streetcar and rode south, rode until I could see no more black faces on the sidewalks. I had now crossed the boundary line of the Black Belt and had entered that territory where jobs were perhaps to be had from white folks. I walked the streets and looked into shop windows until I saw a sign in a delicatessen: PORTER WANTED.

I went in and a stout white woman came to me.

"Vat do you vant?" she asked.

The voice jarred me. She's Jewish, I thought, remembering with shame the obscenities I used to shout at Jewish storekeepers in Arkansas.

"I thought maybe you needed a porter," I said.

"Meester 'Offman, he eesn't here yet," she said. "Vill you vait?"

3

"Yes, ma'am."

"Seet down."

"No, ma'am. I'll wait outside."

"But eet's cold out zhere," she said.

"That's all right," I said.

She shrugged. I went to the sidewalk. I waited for half an hour in the bitter cold, regretting that I had not remained in the warm store, but unable to go back inside. A bald, stoutish white man went into the store and pulled off his coat. Yes, he was the boss man . . . I went in.

"Zo you vant a job?" he asked.

"Yes, sir," I answered, guessing at the meaning of his words.

"Vhere you vork before?"

"In Memphis, Tennessee."

"My brudder-in-law vorked in Tennessee vonce," he said.

I was hired. The work was easy, but I found to my dismay that I could not understand a third of what was said to me. My slow southern ears were baffled by their clouded, thick accents. One morning Mrs. Hoffman asked me to go to a neighboring store— it was owned by a cousin of hers—and get a can of chicken à la king. I had never heard the phrase before and I asked her to repeat it.

"Don't you know nosing?" she demanded of me.

"If you would write it down for me, I'd know what to get," I ventured timidly.

"I can't vite!" she shouted in a sudden fury. "Vat kinda boy ees you?"

I memorized the separate sounds that she had uttered and went to the neighboring store.

"Mrs. Hoffman wants a can of Cheek Keeng Awr Lar Keeng," I said slowly, hoping that he would not think I was being offensive.

"All vite," he said, after staring at me a moment.

He put a can into a paper bag and gave it to me; outside in the street I opened the bag and read the label: Chicken à La King. I cursed, disgusted with myself. I knew those words. It had been her thick accent that had thrown me off. Yet I was not angry with her for speaking broken English; my English, too, was broken. But why could she not have taken more patience? Only one answer came to my mind. I was black and she did not care. Or so I thought . . . I was persisting in reading my present environment in the light of my old one. I reasoned thus: Though English was my native tongue and America my native land, she, an alien, could operate a store and earn a living in a neighborhood where I could not even live. I reasoned further that she was aware of this and was trying to protect her position against me.

(It was not until I had left the delicatessen job that I saw how grossly I had misread the motives and attitudes of Mr. Hoffman and his wife. I had not yet learned anything that would have helped me to thread my way through these perplexing racial relations. Accepting my environment at its face value, trapped by my own emotions, I kept asking myself what had black people done to bring this crazy world upon them?

(The fact of the separation of white and black was clear to me; it was its effect upon the personalities of people that stumped and dismayed me. I did not feel that I was a threat to anybody; yet, as soon as I had grown old enough to think I had learned that my entire personality, my aspirations had long ago been discounted; that, in a measure, the very meaning of the words I spoke could not be fully understood.

(And when I contemplated the area of No Man's Land into which the Negro mind in America had been shunted I wondered if there had ever existed in all human history a more corroding and devastating attack upon the personalities of men than the idea of racial discrimination. In order to escape the racial attack that went to the roots of my life, I would have gladly accepted

5

any way of life but the one in which I found myself. I would have agreed to live under a system of feudal oppression, not because I preferred feudalism but because I felt that feudalism made use of a limited part of a man, defined him, his rank, his function in society. I would have consented to live under the most rigid type of dictatorship, for I felt that dictatorships, too, defined the use of men, however degrading that use might be.

(While working in Memphis I had stood aghast as Shorty had offered himself to be kicked by the white men; but now, while working in Chicago, I was learning that perhaps even a kick was better than uncertainty . . . I had elected, in my fevered search for honorable adjustment to the American scene, not to submit and in doing so I had embraced the daily horror of anxiety, of tension, of eternal disquiet. I could now sympathize with— though I could never bring myself to approve—those tortured blacks who had given up and had gone to their white tormentors and had said: "Kick me, if that's all there is for me; kick me and let me feel at home, let me have peace!"

(Color hate defined the place of black life as below that of white life; and the black man, responding to the same dreams as the white man, strove to bury within his heart his awareness of this difference because it made him lonely and afraid. Hated by whites and being an organic part of the culture that hated him, the black man grew in turn to hate in himself that which others hated in him. But pride would make him hide his self-hate, for he would not want whites to know that he was so thoroughly conquered by them that his total life was conditioned by their attitude; but in the act of hiding his self-hate, he could not help but hate those who evoked his self-hate in him. So each part of his day would be consumed in a war with himself, a good part of his energy would be spent in keeping control of his unruly emo- tions, emotions which he had not wished to have, but could not help having. Held at bay by the hate of others, preoccupied with his own feelings, he was continuously at war with reality. He became inefficient, less able to see and judge the objective world. And when he reached that state, the white people looked at him and laughed and said:

("Look, didn't I tell you niggers were that way?"

(To solve this tangle of balked emotion, I loaded the empty part of the ship of my personality with fantasies of ambition to keep it from toppling over into the sea of senselessness. Like any other American, I dreamed of going into business and making money; I dreamed of working for a firm that would allow me to advance until I reached an important position; I even dreamed of organizing secret groups of blacks to fight all whites. . . . And if the blacks would not agree to organize, then they would have to be fought. I would end up again with self-hate, but it was now a self-hate that was projected outward upon other blacks. Yet I knew—with that part of my mind that the whites had given me—that none of my dreams was possible. Then I would hate myself for allowing my mind to dwell upon the unattainable. Thus the circle would complete itself.

(Slowly I began to forge in the depths of my mind a mechanism that repressed all the dreams and desires that the Chicago streets, the newspapers, the movies were evoking in me. I was going through a second childhood; a new sense of the limit of the possible was being born in me. What could I dream of that had the barest possibility of coming true? I could think of nothing. And, slowly, it was upon exactly that nothingness that my mind began to dwell, that constant sense of wanting without having, of being hated without reason. A dim notion of what life meant to a Negro in America was coming to consciousness in me, not in terms of external events, lynchings, Jim Crowism, and the endless brutalities, but in terms of crossed-up feeling, of psyche pain. I sensed that Negro life was a sprawling land of unconscious suffering, and there were but few Negroes who knew the meaning of their lives, who could tell their story.)

Word reached me that an examination for postal clerk was impending and at once I filed an application and waited. As the date for the examination drew near, I was faced with another problem. How could I get a free day without losing my job? In the South it would have been an unwise policy for a Negro to have gone to his white boss and asked for time to take an examination for another job. It would have implied that the Negro did not like to work for the white boss, that he felt he was not receiving just consideration and, inasmuch as most jobs that Negroes held in the South involved a personal, paternalistic relationship, he would have been risking an argument that might have led to violence.

I now began to speculate about what kind of man Mr. Hoffman was, and I found that I did not know him; that is, I did not know his basic attitude toward Negroes. If I asked him, would he be sympathetic enough to allow me time off with pay? I needed the money. Perhaps he would say: "Go home and stay home if you don't like this job"? I was not sure of him. I decided, therefore, that I had better not risk it. I would forfeit the money and stay away without telling him.

The examination was scheduled to take place on a Monday; I had been working steadily and I would be too tired to do my best if I took the examination without the benefit of rest. I decided to stay away from the shop Saturday, Sunday, and Monday. But what could I tell Mr. Hoffman? Yes, I would tell him that I had been ill. No, that was too thin. I would tell him that my mother had died in Memphis and that I had gone down to bury her. That lie might work.

I took the examination and when I came to the store on Tuesday Mr. Hoffman was astonished, of course.

"I didn't sink you vould ever come back," he said.

"I'm awfully sorry, Mr. Hoffman."

"Vat happened?"

"My mother died in Memphis and I had to go down and bury her," I lied.

He looked at me, then shook his head.

"Rich, you lie," he said.

"I'm not lying," I lied stoutly.

"You vanted to do somesink, zo you zayed ervay," he said, shrugging.

"No, sir. I'm telling you the truth." I piled another lie upon the first one.

"No. You lie. You disappoint me," he said.

"Well, all I can do is tell you the truth," I lied indignantly.

"Vy didn't you use the phone?"

"I didn't think of it." I told a fresh lie.

"Rich, if your mudder die, you vould tell me," he said.

"I didn't have time. Had to catch the train." I lied yet again.

"Vhere did you get the money?"

"My aunt gave it to me," I said, disgusted that I had to lie and lie again.

"I don't vant a boy vat tells lies," he said.

"I don't lie," I lied passionately to protect my lies.

Mrs. Hoffman joined in and both of them hammered at me.

"Ve know. You come from ze Zouth. You feel you can't tell us ze truth. But ve don't bother you. Ve don't feel like people in ze Zouth. Ve treat you nice, don't ve?" they asked.

"Yes, ma'am," I mumbled.

"Zen vy lie?"

"I'm not lying," I lied with all my strength.

I became angry because I knew that they knew that I was lying. I had lied to protect myself, and then I had to lie to protect my lie. I had met so many white faces that would have violently disapproved of my taking the examination that I could not have risked telling Mr. Hoffman the truth. But how could I now tell him that I had lied because I was so unsure of myself? Lying was bad, but revealing my own sense of insecurity would have been worse. It would have been shameful, and I did not like to feel ashamed.

9

Their attitudes had proved utterly amazing. They were taking time out from their duties in the store to talk to me, and I had never encountered anything like that from whites before. A southern white man would have said: "Get to hell out of here!" or "All right, nigger. Get to work." But no white people had ever stood their ground and probed at me, questioned me at such length. It dawned upon me that they were trying to treat me as an equal, which made it even more impossible for me ever to tell them that I had lied, why I had lied. I felt that if I confessed I would give them a moral advantage over me that would be unbearable.

"All vight, zay and vork," Mr. Hoffman said. "I know you're lying, but I don't care, Rich."

I wanted to quit. He had insulted me. But I liked him in spite of myself. Yes, I had done wrong, but how on earth could I have known the kind of people I was working for? Perhaps Mr. Hoffman would have gladly consented for me to take the examination, but my hopes had been far weaker than my powerful fears.

Working with them from day to day and knowing that they knew I had lied from fear crushed me. I knew that they pitied me and pitied the fear in me. I resolved to quit and risk hunger rather than stay with them. I left the job that following Saturday, not telling them that I would not be back, not possessing the heart to say good-bye. I just wanted to go quickly and have them forget that I had ever worked for them.

After an idle week, I got a job as a dishwasher in a North Side café that had just opened. My boss, a white woman, directed me in unpacking barrels of dishes, setting up new tables, painting, and so on. I had charge of serving breakfast; in the late afternoons I carted trays of food to patrons in the hotel who did not want to come down to eat. My wages were fifteen dollars a week; the hours were long, but I ate my meals on the job.

The cook was an elderly Finnish woman with a sharp, bony face. There were several white waitresses. I was the only Negro in the café. The waitresses were a hard, brisk lot and I was keenly aware of how their attitudes contrasted with those of southern white girls. They had not been taught to keep a gulf between me and themselves; they were relatively free of the heritage of racial hate.

One morning as I was making coffee, Cora came forward with a tray loaded with food and squeezed against me to draw a cup of coffee.

"Pardon me, Richard," she said.

"Oh, that's all right," I said in an even tone.

But I was aware that she was a white girl and that her body was pressed closely against mine, an incident that had never happened to me before in my life, an incident charged with the memory of dread. But she was not conscious of my blackness or of what her actions would have meant in the South. And had I not been born in the South, her trivial act would have been as unnoticed by me as it was by her. As she stood close to me, I could not help thinking that if a southern white girl had wanted to draw a cup of coffee, she would have commanded me to step aside so that she might not come in contact with me. The work of the hot and busy kitchen would have had to cease for the moment so that I could have taken my tainted body far enough away to allow the southern white girl a chance to get a cup of coffee. There lay a deep, emotional safety in knowing that the white girl who was now leaning carelessly against me was not thinking of me, had no deep, vague, irrational fright that made her feel that I was a creature to be avoided at all costs.

One summer morning a white girl came late to work and rushed into the pantry where I was busy. She went into the women's room and changed her clothes; I heard the door open and a second later I was surprised to hear her voice:

11

"Richard, quick! Tie my apron!"

She was standing with her back to me and the strings of her apron dangled loose. There was a moment of indecision on my part, then I took the two loose strings and carried them around her body and brought them again to her back and tied them in a clumsy knot.

"Thanks a million," she said, grasping my hand for a split second, and was gone.

I continued my work, filled with all the possible meanings that that tiny, simple, human event could have meant to any Negro in the South where I had spent most of my hungry days.

I did not feel any admiration for the girls, nor any hate. My attitude was one of abiding and friendly wonder. For the most part I was silent with them, though I knew that I had a firmer grasp of life than most of them. As I worked I listened to their talk and perceived its puzzled, wandering, superficial fumbling with the problems and facts of life. There were many things they wondered about that I could have explained to them, but I never dared.

During my lunch hour, which I spent on a bench in a near-by park, the waitresses would come and sit beside me, talking at random, laughing, joking, smoking cigarettes. I learned about their tawdry dreams, their simple hopes, their home lives, their fear of feeling anything deeply, their sex problems, their husbands. They were an eager, restless, talkative, ignorant bunch, but casually kind and impersonal for all that. They knew nothing of hate and fear, and strove instinctively to avoid all passion.

I often wondered what they were trying to get out of life, but I never stumbled upon a clue, and I doubt if they themselves had any notion. They lived on the surface of their days; their smiles were surface smiles, and their tears were surface tears. Negroes lived a truer and deeper life than they, but I wished that Negroes, too, could live as thoughtlessly, serenely as they. The girls never talked of their feelings; none of them possessed the insight or the emotional equipment to understand themselves or others. How far apart in culture we stood! All my life I had done nothing but feel and cultivate my feelings; all their lives they had done nothing but strive for petty goals, the trivial material prizes of American life. We shared a common tongue, but my language was a different language from theirs.

It was in the psychological distance that separated the races that the deepest meaning of the problem of the Negro lay for me. For these poor, ignorant white girls to have understood my life would have meant nothing short of a vast revolution in theirs. And I was convinced that what they needed to make them complete and grown-up in their living was the inclusion in their personalities of a knowledge of lives such as I lived and suffered containedly.

(As I, in memory, think back now upon those girls and their lives I feel that for white America to understand the significance of the problem of the Negro will take a bigger and tougher America than any we have yet known. I feel that America's past is too shallow, her national character too superficially optimistic, her very morality too suffused with color hate for her to accomplish so vast and complex a task. Culturally the Negro represents a paradox: Though he is an organic part of the nation, he is excluded by the entire tide and direction of American culture. Frankly, it is felt to be right to exclude him, and it is felt to be wrong to admit him freely. Therefore if, within the confines of its present culture, the nation ever seeks to purge itself of its color hate, it will find itself at war with itself, convulsed by a spasm of emotional and moral confusion. If the nation ever finds itself examining its real relation to the Negro, it will find itself doing infinitely more than that; for the anti-Negro attitude of whites represents but a tiny part—though a symbolically significant one —of the moral attitude of the nation. Our too-young and too-new

13

America, lusty because it is lonely, aggressive because it is afraid, insists upon seeing the world in terms of good and bad, the holy and the evil, the high and the low, the white and the black; our America is frightened of fact, of history, of processes, of necessity. It hugs the easy way of damning those whom it cannot understand, of excluding those who look different, and it salves its conscience with a self-draped cloak of righteousness. Am I damning my native land? No; for I, too, share these faults of character! And I really do not think that America, adolescent and cocksure, a stranger to suffering and travail, an enemy of passion and sacrifice, is ready to probe into its most fundamental beliefs.

(I know that not race alone, not color alone, but the daily values that give meaning to life stood between me and those white girls with whom I worked. Their constant outward-looking, their mania for radios, cars, and a thousand other trinkets made them dream and fix their eyes upon the trash of life, made it impossible for them to learn a language which could have taught them to speak of what was in their or others' hearts. The words of their souls were the syllables of popular songs.

(The essence of the irony of the plight of the Negro in America, to me, is that he is doomed to live in isolation while those who condemn him seek the basest goals of any people on the face of the earth. Perhaps it would be possible for the Negro to become reconciled to his plight if he could be made to believe that his sufferings were for some remote, high, sacrificial end; but sharing the culture that condemns him, and seeing that a lust for trash is what blinds the nation to his claims, is what sets storms to rolling in his soul.)

Though I had fled the pressure of the South, my outward conduct had not changed. I had been schooled to present an unalteringly smiling face and I continued to do so despite the fact that my environment allowed more open expression. I hid my feelings and avoided all relationships with whites that might cause me to reveal them.

One afternoon the boss lady entered the kitchen and found me sitting on a box reading a copy of the *American Mercury*.

"What on earth are you reading?" she demanded.

I was at once on guard, though I knew I did not have to be.

"Oh, just a magazine," I said.

"Where did you get it?" she asked.

"Oh, I just found it," I lied; I had bought it.

"Do you understand it?" she asked.

"Yes, ma'am."

"Well," she exclaimed, "the colored dishwasher reads the *American Mercury!*"

She walked away, shaking her head. My feelings were mixed. I was glad that she had learned that I was not completely dumb, yet I felt a little angry because she seemed to think it odd for dishwashers to read magazines. Thereafter I kept my books and magazines wrapped in newspaper so that no one would see them, reading them at home and on the streetcar to and from work.

Tillie, the Finnish cook, was a tall, ageless, red-faced, rawboned woman with long, snow-white hair which she balled in a knot at the nape of her neck. She cooked expertly and was superbly efficient. One morning as I passed the sizzling stove I thought I heard Tillie cough and spit. I paused and looked carefully to see where her spittle had gone, but I saw nothing; her face, obscured by steam, was bent over a big pot. My senses told me that Tillie had coughed and spat into that pot, but my heart told me that no human being could possibly be so filthy. I decided to watch her. An hour or so later I heard Tillie clear her throat with a grunt, saw her cough, and spit into the boiling soup. I held my breath; I did not want to believe what I had seen.

Should I tell the boss lady? Would she believe me? I watched Tillie for another day to make sure that she was spitting into the food. She was; there was no doubt of it. But who would believe me if I told them what was happening? I was the only black person in the café. Perhaps they would think that I hated the cook? I stopped eating my meals there and bided my time.

The business of the café was growing rapidly and a Negro girl was hired to make salads. I went to her at once.

"Look, can I trust you?" I asked.

"What are you talking about?" she asked.

"I want you to say nothing, but watch that cook."

"For what?"

"Now, don't get scared. Just watch the cook."

She looked at me as though she thought I was crazy; and, frankly, I felt that perhaps I ought not to say anything to anybody.

"What do you mean?" she demanded.

"All right," I said. "I'll tell you. That cook spits in the food."

"What are you saying?" she asked aloud.

"Keep quiet," I said.

"Spitting?" she asked me in a whisper. "Why would she do that?"

"I don't know. But watch her."

She walked away from me with a funny look in her eyes. But half an hour later she came rushing to me, looking ill, sinking into a chair.

"Oh, God, I feel awful!"

"Did you see it?"

"She *is* spitting in the food!"

"What ought we do?" I asked.

"Tell the lady," she said.

"She wouldn't believe me," I said.

She widened her eyes as she understood. We were black and the cook was white.

"But I can't work here if she's going to do that," she said.

"Then you tell her," I said.

"She wouldn't believe me either," she said.

She rose and ran to the women's room. When she returned she stared at me. We were two Negroes and we were silently asking ourselves if the white boss lady would believe us if we told her that her expert white cook was spitting in the food all day long as it cooked upon the stove.

"I don't know," she wailed in a whisper and walked away.

I thought of telling the waitresses about the cook, but I could not get up enough nerve. Many of the girls were friendly with Tillie. Yet I could not let the cook spit in the food all day. That was wrong by any human standard of conduct. I washed dishes, thinking, wondering; I served breakfast, thinking, wondering; I served meals in the apartments of patrons upstairs, thinking, wondering. Each time I picked up a tray of food I felt like retching. Finally the Negro salad girl came to me and handed me her purse and hat.

"I'm going to tell her and quit, goddamn," she said.

"I'll quit too, if she doesn't fire her," I said.

"Oh, she won't believe me," she wailed in agony.

"You tell her. You're a woman. She might believe you."

Her eyes welled with tears and she sat for a long time; then she rose and went abruptly into the dining room. I went to the door and peered. Yes, she was at the desk, talking to the boss lady. She returned to the kitchen and went into the pantry; I followed her.

"Did you tell her?" I asked.

"Yes."

"What did she say?"

"She said I was crazy."

"Oh, God!" I said.

"She just looked at me with those gray eyes of hers," the girl said. "Why would Tillie do that?"

"I don't know," I said.

The boss lady came to the door and called the girl; both of

them went into the dining room. Tillie came over to me; a hard cold look was in her eyes.

"What's happening here?" she asked.

"I don't know," I said, wanting to slap her across the mouth.

She muttered something and went back to the stove, coughed, spat into a bubbling pot. I left the kitchen and went into the back areaway to breathe. The boss lady came out.

"Richard," she said.

Her face was pale, I was smoking a cigarette and I did not look at her.

"Is this true?"

"Yes, ma'am."

"It couldn't be. Do you know what you're saying?"

"Just watch her," I said.

"I don't know," she moaned.

She looked crushed. She went back into the dining room, but I saw her watching the cook through the doors. I watched both of them, the boss lady and the cook, praying that the cook would spit again. She did. The boss lady came into the kitchen and stared at Tillie, but she did not utter a word. She burst into tears and ran back into the dining room.

"What's happening here?" Tillie demanded.

No one answered. The boss lady came out and tossed Tillie her hat, coat, and money.

"Now, get out of here, you dirty dog!" she said.

Tillie stared, then slowly picked up her hat, coat, and the money; she stood a moment, wiped sweat from her forehead with her hand, then spat, this time on the floor. She left.

Nobody was ever able to fathom why Tillie liked to spit into the food.

Brooding over Tillie, I recalled the time when the boss man in Mississippi had come to me and had tossed my wages to me and said:

18

"Get out, nigger! I don't like your looks."

And I wondered if a Negro who did not smile and grin was as morally loathsome to whites as a cook who spat into the food. . . .

I worked at the café all spring and in June I was called for temporary duty in the post office. My confidence soared; if I obtained an appointment as a regular clerk, I could spend at least five hours a day writing.

I reported at the post office and was sworn in as a temporary clerk. I earned seventy cents an hour and I went to bed each night now with a full stomach for the first time in my life. When I worked nights, I wrote during the day; when I worked days, I wrote during the night.

But the happiness of having a job did not keep another worry from rising to plague me. Before I could receive a permanent appointment I would have to take a physical examination. The weight requirement was one hundred and twenty-five pounds and I—with my long years of semistarvation—barely tipped the scales at a hundred and ten. Frantically I turned all of my spare money into food and ate. But my skin and flesh would not respond to the food. Perhaps I was not eating the right diet? Perhaps my chronic anxiety kept my weight down. I drank milk, ate steak, but it did not give me an extra ounce of flesh. I visited a doctor who told me that there was nothing wrong with me except malnutrition, that I must eat and sleep long hours. I did and my weight remained the same. I knew now that my job was temporary and that when the time came for my appointment I would have to resume my job hunting again.

At night I read Stein's *Three Lives,* Crane's *The Red Badge of Courage,* and Dostoevski's *The Possessed,* all of which revealed new realms of feeling. But the most important discoveries came when I veered from fiction proper into the field of psychology and sociology. I ran through volumes that bore upon the causes of my conduct and the conduct of my people. I studied tables of figures relating population density to insanity, relating housing to disease, relating school and recreational opportunities to crime, relating various forms of neurotic behavior to environment, relating racial insecurities to the conflicts between whites and blacks . . .

I still had no friends, casual or intimate, and felt the need for none. I had developed a self-sufficiency that kept me distant from others, emotionally and psychologically. Occasionally I went to house-rent parties, parties given by working-class families to raise money to pay the landlord, the admission to which was a quarter or a half dollar. At these affairs I drank home-brewed beer, ate spaghetti and chitterlings, laughed and talked with black, south-ern-born girls who worked as domestic servants in white middle-class homes. But with none of them did my relations rest upon my deepest feelings. I discussed what I read with no one, and to none did I confide. Emotionally, I was withdrawn from the objec-tive world; my desires floated loosely within the walls of my consciousness, contained and controlled.

As a protective mechanism, I developed a terse, cynical mode of speech that rebuffed those who sought to get too close to me. Conversation was my way of avoiding expression; my words were reserved for those times when I sat down alone to write. My face was always a deadpan or a mask of general friendliness; no word or event could jar me into a gesture of enthusiasm or despair. A slowly, hesitantly spoken "Yeah" was my general verbal reaction to almost everything I heard. "That's pretty good," said with a slow nod of the head, was my approval. "Aw, naw," muttered with a cold smile, was my rejection. Even though I reacted deeply, my true feelings raced along underground, hidden.

I did not act in this fashion deliberately; I did not prefer this kind of relationship with people. I wanted a life in which there was a constant oneness of feeling with others, in which the basic emotions of life were shared, in which common memory formed a common past, in which collective hope reflected a national future. But I knew that no such thing was possible in my environment. The only ways in which I felt that my feelings could go outward without fear of rude rebuff or searing reprisal was in writing or reading, and to me they were ways of living.

Aunt Maggie had now rented an apartment in which I shared a rear room. My mother and brother came and all three of us slept in that one room; there was no window, just four walls and a door. My excessive reading puzzled Aunt Maggie; she sensed my fiercely indrawn nature and she did not like it. Being of an open, talkative disposition, she declared that I was going about the business of living wrongly, that reading books would not help me at all. But nothing she said had any effect. I had long ago hardened myself to criticism.

"Boy, are you reading for law?" my aunt would demand.

"No."

"Then why are you reading all the time?"

"I like to."

"But what do you get out of it?"

"I get a great deal out of it."

And I knew that my words sounded wild and foolish in my environment, where reading was almost unknown, where the highest item of value was a dime or a dollar, an apartment or a job; where, if one aspired at all, it was to be a doctor or a lawyer, a shopkeeper or a politician. The most valued pleasure of the people I knew was a car, the most cherished experience a bottle of whisky, the most sought-after prize somebody else's wife. I had no sense of being inferior or superior to the people about me; I merely felt that they had had no chance to learn to live differently. I never criticized them or praised them, yet they felt in my neutrality a deeper rejection of them than if I had cursed them.

Repeatedly I took stabs at writing, but the results were so poor that I would tear up the sheets. I was striving for a level of expression that matched those of the novels I read. But I always somehow failed to get onto the page what I thought and felt. Failing at sustained narrative, I compromised by playing with single sentences and phrases. Under the influence of Stein's *Three Lives*, I spent hours and days pounding out disconnected sentences for the sheer love of words.

I would write:

"The soft melting hunk of butter trickled in gold down the stringy grooves of the split yam."

Or:

"The child's clumsy fingers fumbled in sleep, feeling vainly for the wish of its dream."

"The old man huddled in the dark doorway, his bony face lit by the burning yellow in the windows of distant skyscrapers."

My purpose was to capture a physical state or movement that carried a strong subjective impression, an accomplishment which seemed supremely worth struggling for. If I could fasten the mind of the reader upon words so firmly that he would forget words and be conscious only of his response, I felt that I would be in sight of knowing how to write narrative. I strove to master words, to make them disappear, to make them important by making them new, to make them melt into a rising spiral of emotional stimuli, each greater than the other, each feeding and reinforcing the other, and all ending in an emotional climax that would drench the reader with a sense of a new world. That was the single aim of my living.

Autumn came and I was called for my physical examination for the position of regular postal clerk. I had not told my mother or brother or aunt that I knew I would fail. On the morning of the examination I drank two quarts of buttermilk, ate six bananas, but it did not hoist the red arrow of the government scales to the required mark of one hundred and twenty-five pounds. I went home and sat disconsolately in my back room, hating myself, wondering where I could find another job. I had almost got my hands upon a decent job and had lost it, had let it slip through my fingers. Waves of self-doubt rose to haunt me. Was I always to hang on the fringes of life? What I wanted was truly modest, and yet my past, my diet, my hunger, had snatched it from before my eyes. But these self-doubts did not last long; I dulled the sense of loss through reading, reading, writing and more writing.

The loss of my job did not evoke in me any hostility toward the system of rules that had barred my first grasp at the material foundations of American life. I felt that it was unfair that my lack of a few pounds of flesh should deprive me of a chance at a good job, but I had long ago emotionally rejected the world in which I lived and my reaction was: Well, this is the system by which people want the world to run whether it helps them or not. To me, my losing was only another manifestation of that queer, material way of American living that computed everything in terms of the concrete: weight, color, race, fur coats, radios, electric refrigerators, cars, money . . . It seemed that I simply could not fit into a materialistic life.

The living arrangement of my mother, brother, and Aunt Maggie—now that I had no promise of being a postal clerk—quickly deteriorated. In Aunt Maggie's eyes I was a plainly marked failure and she feared that perhaps she would have to feed me. The emotional atmosphere in the cramped quarters became tense, ugly, petty, bickering. Fault was found with my reading and writing; it was claimed that I was swelling the electric bill. Though I had saved almost no money, I decided to rent an apartment. Aunt Cleo was living in a rented room and I invited her to share the apartment with me, my mother, and brother, and she consented. We moved into a tiny, dingy two-room den in whose kitchen a wall bed fitted snugly into a corner near the stove. The place was alive with vermin and the smell of cooking hung in the air day and night.

I asked for my job back at the café and the boss lady allowed me to return; again I served breakfast, washed dishes, carted trays of food up into the apartments. Another postal examination was scheduled for spring and to that end I made eating an obsession. I ate when I did not want to eat, drank milk when it sickened me. Slowly my starved body responded to food and overcame the lean years of Mississippi, Arkansas, and Tennessee, counteracting the flesh-sapping anxiety of fear-filled days.

I read Proust's *A Remembrance of Things Past,* admiring the lucid, subtle but strong prose, stupefied by its dazzling magic, awed by the vast, delicate, intricate, and psychological structure of the Frenchman's epic of death and decadence. But it crushed me with hopelessness, for I wanted to write of the people in my environment with an equal thoroughness, and the burning example before my eyes made me feel that I never could.

My ability to endure tension had now grown amazingly. From the accidental pain of southern years, from anxiety that I had sought to avoid, from fear that had been too painful to bear, I had learned to like my unintermittent burden of feeling, had become habituated to acting with all of my being, had learned to seek those areas of life, those situations, where I knew that events would complement my own inner mood. I was conscious of what was happening to me; I knew that my attitude of watchful wonder had usurped all other feelings, had become the meaning of my life, an integral part of my personality; that I was striving to live and measure all things by it. Having no claims upon others, I bent the way the wind blew, rendering unto my environment that which was my environment's, and rendering unto myself that which I felt was mine.

It was a dangerous way to live, far more dangerous than violating laws or ethical codes of conduct; but the danger was for me and me alone. Had I not been conscious of what I was doing, I could have easily lost my way in the fogbound regions of compelling fantasy. Even so, I floundered, staggered; but somehow I always groped my way back to that path where I felt a tinge of warmth from an unseen light.

Hungry for insight into my own life and the lives about me, knowing my fiercely indrawn nature, I sought to fulfill more than my share of all obligations and responsibilities, as though offering libations of forgiveness to my environment. Indeed, the more my emotions claimed my attention, the sharper—as though in ultimate self-defense—became my desire to measure accurately the reality of the objective world so that I might more than meet its demands. At twenty years of age the mold of my life was set, was hardening into a pattern, a pattern that was neither good nor evil, neither right nor wrong.

# Chapter II

I N the spring I took the postal examination again. Time had somewhat repaired the ravages of hunger and I was able to meet the required physical weight. We moved to a larger apartment. My increased pay made better food possible. I was happy in my own way.

Working nights, I spent my days in experimental writing, filling endless pages with stream-of-consciousness Negro dialect, trying to depict the dwellers of the Black Belt as I felt and saw them. My reading in sociology had enabled me to discern many strange types of Negro characters, to identify many modes of Negro behavior; and what moved me above all was the frequency of mental illness, that tragic toll that the urban environment exacted of the black peasant. Perhaps my writing was more an attempt at understanding than self-expression. A need that I did not comprehend made me use words to create religious types, criminal types, the warped, the lost, the baffled; my pages were full of tension, frantic poverty, and death.

But something was missing in my imaginative efforts; my flights of imagination were too subjective, too lacking in reference to social action. I hungered for a grasp of the framework of contemporary living, for a knowledge of the forms of life about me, for eyes to see the bony structures of personality, for theories to light up the shadows of conduct.

While sorting mail in the post office, I met a young Irish chap whose sensibilities amazed me. We would take a batch of mail in our fingers and, while talking in low monotones out of the sides of our mouths, toss them correctly into their designated holes and suddenly our hands would be empty and we would have no memory of having worked. Most of the clerks could work in this automatic manner. The Irish chap and I had read a lot in common and we laughed at the same sacred things. He was as cynical as I was regarding uplift and hope, and we were proud of having escaped what we called the "childhood disease of metaphysical fear." I was introduced to the Irish chap's friends and we formed a "gang" of Irish, Jewish, and Negro wits who poked fun at government, the masses, statesmen, and political parties. We assumed that all people were good to the degree to which they amused us, or to the extent to which we could make them objects of laughter. We ridiculed all ideas of protest, of organized rebellion or revolution. We felt that all businessmen were thoroughly stupid and that no other group was capable of rising to challenge them. We sneered at voting, for we felt that the choice between one political crook and another was too small for serious thought. We believed that man should live by hard facts alone, and we had so long ago put God out of our minds that we did not even discuss Him.

During this cynical period I met a Negro literary group on Chicago's South Side; it was composed of a dozen or more boys and girls, all of whom possessed academic learning, economic freedom, and vague ambitions to write. I found them more formal in manner than their white counterparts; they wore stylish clothes and were finicky about their personal appearance. I had naïvely supposed that I would have much in common with them, but I found them preoccupied with twisted sex problems. Coming from a station in life which they no doubt would have branded "lower class," I could not understand why they were so all-absorbed with sexual passion. I was encountering for the first time the full-fledged Negro Puritan invert—the emotionally sick—and I discovered that their ideas were but excuses for sex, leads to sex, hints at sex, substitutes for sex. In speech and action they strove to act as un-Negro as possible, denying the racial and material foundations of their lives, accepting their class and racial status in ways so oblique that one had the impression that no difficulties existed for them. Though I had never had any assignments from a college professor, I had made much harder and more prolonged attempts at self-expression than any of them. Swearing love for art, they hovered on the edge of Bohemian life. Always friendly, they could never be anybody's friend; always reading, they could really never learn; always boasting of their passions, they could never really feel and were afraid to live.

The one group I met during those exploring days whose lives enthralled me was the Garveyites, an organization of black men and women who were forlornly seeking to return to Africa. Theirs was a passionate rejection of America, for they sensed with that directness of which only the simple are capable that they had no chance to live a full human life in America. Their lives were not cluttered with ideas in which they could only half believe; they could not create illusions which made them think they were living when they were not; their daily lives were too nakedly harsh to permit of camouflage. I understood their emotions, for I partly shared them.

The Garveyites had embraced a totally racialistic outlook which endowed them with a dignity that I had never seen before in Negroes. On the walls of their dingy flats were maps of Africa and India and Japan, pictures of Japanese generals and admirals, portraits of Marcus Garvey in gaudy regalia, the faces of colored men and women from all parts of the world. I gave no credence to the ideology of Garveyism; it was, rather, the emotional dynamics of its adherents that evoked my admiration. Those Garveyites I knew could never understand why I liked them but would never

28

follow them, and I pitied them too much to tell them that they could never achieve their goal, that Africa was owned by the imperial powers of Europe, that their lives were alien to the mores of the natives of Africa, that they were people of the West and would forever be so until they either merged with the West or perished. It was when the Garveyites spoke fervently of building their own country, of someday living within the boundaries of a culture of their own making, that I sensed the passionate hunger of their lives, that I caught a glimpse of the potential strength of the American Negro.

Rumors of unemployment came, but I did not listen to them. I heard of the organizational efforts of the Communist party among the Negroes of the South Side, but Communist activities were too remote to strike my mind with any degree of vividness. Whenever I met a person whom I suspected of being a Communist, I talked to him affably but from an emotional distance. I sensed that something terrible was beginning to happen in the world, but I tried to shut it out of my mind by reading and writing.

When the time came for my appointment as a regular clerk, I was told that no appointments would be made for the time being. The volume of mail dropped. My hours of work dwindled. My paychecks grew small. Food became scarce at home. The hunger I thought I had left behind returned. One winter afternoon, in 1929, en route to work from the library, I passed a newsstand on which papers blazed:

## Stocks Crash—Billions Fade

Most of what I had seen in newspapers had never concerned me, so why should this? Newspapers reported the doings in a life I did not share. But the volume of mail fell so low that I worked but one or two nights a week. In the post-office canteen the boys stood about and talked.

"The cops beat up some demonstrators today."

"The Reds had a picket line around the City Hall."

"Wall Street's cracking down on the country."

"Surplus production's throwing millions out of work."

"There're more than two million unemployed."

"They don't count. They're always out of work."

"Read Karl Marx and get the answer, boys."

"There'll be a revolution if this keeps up."

"Hell, naw. Americans are too dumb to make a revolution."

The post-office job ended and again I was out of work. I could no longer think that the tides of economics were not my concern. But how could I have had any possible say in how the world had been run? I had grown up in complete ignorance of what created jobs. Having been thrust out of the world because of my race, I had accepted my destiny by not being curious about what shaped it.

The following summer I was again called for temporary duty in the post office, and the work lasted into the winter. Aunt Cleo succumbed to a severe cardiac condition and, hard on the heels of her illness, my brother developed stomach ulcers. To rush my worries to a climax, my mother also became ill. I felt that I was maintaining a private hospital. Finally the post-office work ceased altogether and I haunted the city for jobs. But when I went into the streets in the morning I saw sights that killed my hope for the rest of the day. Unemployed men loitered in doorways with blank looks in their eyes, sat dejectedly on front steps in shabby clothing, congregated in sullen groups on street corners, and filled all the empty benches in the parks of Chicago's South Side.

Luck of a sort came when a distant cousin of mine, who was a superintendent in a Negro burial society, offered me a position on his staff as an agent. The thought of selling insurance policies to ignorant Negroes disgusted me.

"Well, if you don't sell them, somebody else will," my cousin told me. "You've got to eat, haven't you?"

During that year I worked for several burial and insurance societies that operated among Negroes, and I received a new kind of education. I found that the burial societies, with some exceptions, were mostly "rackets." Some of them conducted their businesses legitimately, but there were many that exploited the ignorance of their black customers.

I was paid under a system that netted me fifteen dollars for every dollar's worth of new premiums that I placed upon the company's books, and for every dollar's worth of old premiums that lapsed I was penalized fifteen dollars. In addition, I was paid a commission of ten per cent on total premiums collected, but during the depression it was extremely difficult to persuade a black family to buy a policy carrying even a dime premium. I considered myself lucky if, after subtracting lapses from new business, there remained fifteen dollars that I could call my own.

This "gambling" method of remuneration was practiced by some of the burial companies because of the tremendous "turnover" in policyholders, and the companies had to have a constant stream of new business to keep afloat. Whenever a black family moved or suffered a slight reverse in fortune, it usually let its policy lapse and later bought another policy from some other company.

Each day now I saw how the Negro in Chicago lived, for I visited hundreds of dingy flats filled with rickety furniture and ill-clad children. Most of the policyholders were illiterate and did not know that their policies carried clauses severely restricting their benefit payments, and, as an insurance agent, it was not my duty to tell them.

After tramping the streets and pounding on doors to collect premiums, I was dry, strained, too tired to read or write. I hungered for relief and, as a salesman of insurance to many young

31

black girls, I found it. There were many comely black housewives who, trying desperately to keep up their insurance payments, were willing to make bargains to escape paying a ten-cent premium each week. She was an illiterate black child with a baby whose father she did not know. During the entire period of my relationship with her, she had but one demand to make of me: She wanted me to take her to a circus. Just what significance circuses had for her, I was never able to learn.

After I had been with her one morning—in exchange for the dime premium—I sat on the sofa in the front room and began to read a book I had with me. She came over shyly.

"Lemme see that," she said.

"What?" I asked.

"That book," she said.

I gave her the book; she looked at it intently. I saw that she was holding it upside down.

"What's in here you keep reading?" she asked.

"Can't you really read?" I asked.

"Naw," she giggled. "You know I can't read."

"You can read *some,*" I said.

"Naw," she said.

I stared at her and wondered just what a life like hers meant in the scheme of things, and I came to the conclusion that it meant absolutely nothing. And neither did my life mean anything.

"How come you looking at me that way for?"

"Nothing."

"You don't talk much."

"There isn't much to say."

"I wished Jim was here," she sighed.

"Who's Jim?" I asked, jealous. I knew that she had other men, but I resented her mentioning them in my presence.

"Just a friend," she said.

I hated her then, then hated myself for coming to her.

"Do you like Jim better than you like me?" I asked.

"Naw. Jim just likes to talk."

"Then why do you be with me, if you like Jim better?" I asked, trying to make an issue and feeling a wave of disgust because I wanted to.

"You all right," she said, giggling. "I like you."

"I could kill you," I said.

"What?" she exclaimed.

"Nothing," I said, ashamed.

"Kill me, you said? You crazy, man," she said.

"Maybe I am," I muttered, angry that I was sitting beside a human being to whom I could not talk, angry with myself for coming to her, hating my wild and restless loneliness.

"You oughta go home and sleep," she said. "You tired."

"What do you ever think about?" I demanded harshly.

"Lotta things."

"What, for example?"

"You," she said, smiling.

"You know I mean just one dime to you each week," I said.

"Naw, I thinka lotta you."

"Then what do you think?"

" 'Bout how you talk when you talk. I wished I could talk like you," she said seriously.

"Why?" I taunted her.

"When you gonna take me to a circus?" she demanded suddenly.

"You ought to be in a circus," I said.

"I'd like it," she said, her eyes shining.

I wanted to laugh, but her words sounded so sincere that I could not laugh.

"There's no circus in town," I said.

"I bet there is and you won't tell me 'cause you don't wanna take me," she said, pouting.

"But there's no circus in town, I tell you!"

"When will one come?"

"I don't know."

"Can't you read it in the papers?" she asked.

"There's nothing in the papers about a circus."

"There is," she said. "If I could read, I'd find it."

I laughed and she was hurt.

"There *is* a circus in town," she said stoutly.

"There's no circus in town," I said. "But if you want to learn to read, then I'll teach you."

She nestled at my side, giggling.

"See that word?" I said, pointing.

"Yeah."

"That's an 'and,' " I said.

She doubled, giggling.

"What's the matter?" I asked.

She rolled on the floor, giggling.

"What's so funny?" I demanded.

"You," she giggled. "You so funny."

I rose.

"The hell with you," I said.

"Don't you go and cuss me now," she said. "I don't cuss you."

"I'm sorry," I said.

I got my hat and went to the door.

"I'll see you next week?" she asked.

"Maybe," I said.

When I was on the sidewalk, she called to me from a window.

"You promised to take me to a circus, remember?"

"Yes." I walked close to the window. "What is it you like about a circus?"

"The animals," she said simply.

I felt that there was a hidden meaning, perhaps, in what she had said; but I could not find it. She laughed and slammed the window shut.

Each time I left her I resolved not to visit her again. I could not talk to her; I merely listened to her passionate desire to see a circus. She was not calculating; if she liked a man, she just liked him. Sex relations were the only relations she had ever had; no others were possible with her, so limited was her intelligence.

Most of the other agents also had their bought girls and they were extremely anxious to keep other agents from tampering with them. One day a new section of the South Side was given to me as a part of my collection area and the agent from whom the territory had been taken suddenly became very friendly with me.

"Say, Wright," he asked, "did you collect from Ewing at ——— Champlain Avenue yet?"

"Yes," I answered, after consulting my book.

"How did you like her?" he asked, staring at me.

"She's a good-looking number," I said.

"You had anything to do with her yet?" he asked.

"No, but I'd like to," I said, laughing.

"Look," he said. "I'm a friend of yours."

"Since when?" I countered.

"No, I'm really a friend," he said.

"What's on your mind?"

"Listen, that gal's sick," he said seriously.

"What do you mean?"

"She's got the clap," he said. "Keep away from her. She'll lay with anybody."

"Gee, I'm glad you told me," I said.

"You had your eye on her, didn't you?" he asked.

"Yes, I did," I said.

"Leave her alone," he said. "She'll get you down."

That night I told my cousin what the agent had said about Miss Ewing. My cousin laughed.

"That gal's all right," he said. "That agent's been fooling around with her. He told you she had a disease so that you'd be scared to bother her. He was protecting her from you."

That was the way the black women were regarded by the black agents. Some of the agents were vicious; if they had claims to pay to a sick black woman and if the woman was able to have sex relations with them, they would insist upon it, using the claim money as a bribe. If the woman refused, they would report to the office that the woman was a malingerer. The average black woman would submit because she needed the money badly.

As an insurance agent, it was necessary for me to take part in one swindle. It appears that the burial society had originally issued a policy that was—from their point of view—too liberal in its provisions, and the officials decided to exchange the policies then in the hands of their clients for other policies carrying stricter clauses; of course, this had to be done in a manner that would not allow the policyholder to know that his policy was being switched, that he was being swindled. I did not like it, but there was only one thing I could do to keep from being a party to it: I could quit and starve. But I did not feel that being honest was worth the price of starvation.

The swindle worked in this way. In my visits to the homes of policyholders to collect premiums, I was accompanied by the superintendent who claimed to the policyholder that he was making a routine inspection. The policyholder, usually an illiterate black woman, would dig up her policy from the bottom of a trunk or a chest and hand it to the superintendent. Meanwhile I would be marking the woman's premium book, an act which would distract her from what the superintendent was doing. The superintendent would exchange the old policy for a new one which was identical in color, serial number, and beneficiary, but which carried much smaller payments. It was dirty work and I wondered how I could stop it. And when I could think of no safe way I would curse myself and the victims and forget about it. (The black owners of the burial societies were leaders in the Negro communities and were respected by whites.)

As I went from house to house collecting money, I saw black men mounted upon soapboxes at street corners, bellowing about bread, rights, and revolution. I liked their courage, but I doubted their wisdom. The speakers claimed that Negroes were angry, that they were about to rise and join their white fellow workers to make a revolution. I was in and out of many Negro homes each day and I knew that the Negroes were lost, ignorant, sick in mind and body. I saw that a vast distance separated the agitators from the masses, a distance so vast that the agitators did not know how to appeal to the people they sought to lead.

Some mornings I found leaflets on my steps telling of China, Russia, and Germany; on some days I witnessed as many as five thousand jobless Negroes, led by Communists, surging through the streets. I would watch them with an aching heart, firmly convinced that they were being duped; but if I had been asked to give them another solution for their problems, I would not have known how.

It became a habit of mine to visit Washington Park of an afternoon after collecting a part of my premiums, and I would wander through crowds of unemployed Negroes, pausing here and there to sample the dialectic or indignation of Communist speakers. What I heard and saw baffled and angered me. The Negro Communists were deliberately careless in their personal appearance, wearing their shirt collars turned in to make V's at their throats, wearing their caps—they wore caps because Lenin had worn caps—with the visors turned backward, tilted upward at the nape of their necks. Many of their mannerisms, pronunciations, and turns of speech had been consciously copied from white Communists whom they had recently met. While engaged in conversation, they stuck their thumbs in their suspenders or put their left hands into their shirt bosoms or hooked their thumbs into their back pockets as they had seen Lenin or Stalin do in photographs. Though they did not know it, they were naïvely practicing magic; they thought that if they acted like the men who had overthrown the czar, then surely they ought to be able to win their freedom in America.

In speaking they rolled their "r's" in Continental style, pronouncing "party" as "parrrtee," stressing the last syllable, having picked up the habit from white Communists. "Comrades" became "cumrrrades," and "distribute," which they had known how to pronounce all their lives, was twisted into "distrrribuuute," with the accent on the last instead of the second syllable, a mannerism which they copied from Polish Communist immigrants who did not know how to pronounce the word. Many sensitive Negroes agreed with the Communist program but refused to join their ranks because of the shabby quality of those Negroes whom the Communists had already admitted to membership.

When speaking from the platform, the Negro Communists, eschewing the traditional gestures of the Negro preacher—as though they did not possess the strength to develop their own style of Communist preaching—stood straight, threw back their heads, brought the edge of the right palm down hammerlike into the outstretched left palm in a series of jerky motions to pound their points home, a mannerism that characterized Lenin's method of speaking. When they walked, their stride quickened; all the peasant hesitancy of their speech vanished as their voices became clipped, terse. In debate they interrupted their opponents in a tone of voice that was an octave higher, and if their opponents raised their voices to be heard, the Communists raised theirs still higher until shouts rang out over the park. Hence, the only truth that prevailed was that which could be shouted and quickly understood.

Their emotional certainty seemed buttressed by access to a fund of knowledge denied to ordinary men, but a day's observation of their activities was sufficient to reveal all their thought processes. An hour's listening disclosed the fanatical intolerance

38

of minds sealed against new ideas, new facts, new feelings, new attitudes, new hints at ways to live. They denounced books they had never read, people they had never known, ideas they could never understand, and doctrines whose names they could not pronounce. Communism, instead of making them leap forward with fire in their hearts to become masters of ideas and life, had frozen them at an even lower level of ignorance than had been theirs before they met Communism.

When Hoover threatened to drive the bonus marchers from Washington, one Negro Communist speaker said:

"If he drives the bonus marchers out of Washington, the people will rise up and make a revolution!"

I went to him, determined to get at what he really meant.

"You know that even if the United States army actually kills the bonus marchers, there'll be no revolution," I said.

"You don't know the indignation of the masses!" he exploded.

"But you don't seem to know what it takes to make a revolution," I explained. "Revolutions are rare occurrences."

"You underestimate the masses," he told me.

"No, I know the masses of Negroes very well," I said. "But I don't believe that a revolution is pending. Revolutions come through concrete historical processes . . ."

"You're an intellectual," he said, smiling disdainfully.

A few days later, after Hoover had had the bonus marchers driven from Washington at the point of bayonets, I accosted him:

"What about that revolution you predicted if the bonus marchers were driven out?" I asked.

"The prerequisite conditions did not exist," he muttered, and shrugged.

I left him, wondering why he felt it necessary to make so many ridiculous overstatements. I could not refute the general Communist analysis of the world; the only drawback was that their world was just too simple for belief. I liked their readiness to act, but they seemed lost in folly, wandering in a fantasy. For them there was no yesterday or tomorrow, only the living moment of today; their only task was to annihilate the enemy that confronted them in any manner possible.

At times their speeches, glowing with rebellions, were downright offensive to lowly, hungry Negroes. Once a Negro Communist speaker, inveighing against religion, said:

"There ain't no goddamn God! If there is, I hereby challenge Him to strike me dead!"

He paused dramatically before his vast black audience for God to act, but God declined. He then pulled out his watch.

"Maybe God didn't hear me!" he yelled. "I'll give Him two more minutes!" Then, with sarcasm: "Mister God, kill me!"

He waited, looking mockingly at his watch. The audience laughed uneasily.

"I'll tell you where to find God," the speaker went on in a hard, ranting voice. "When it rains at midnight, take your hat, turn it upside down on a floor in a dark room, and you'll have God!"

I had to admit that I had never heard atheism of so militant a nature; but the Communist speaker seemed to be amusing and frightening the people more than he was convincing them.

"If there is a God up there in that empty sky," the speaker roared on, "I'll reach up there and grab Him by his beard and jerk Him down here on this hungry earth and cut His throat!" He wagged his head. "Now, let God dare me!"

The audience was shocked into silence for a moment, then it yelled with delight. I shook my head and walked away. That was not the way to destroy people's outworn beliefs . . . They were acting like irresponsible children . . .

I was now convinced that they did not know the complex nature of Negro life, did not know how great was the task to which they had set themselves. They had rejected the state of things as they were, and that seemed to me to be the first step toward embracing a creative attitude toward life. I felt that it was not until one wanted the world to be different that one could look at the world with will and emotion. But these men had rejected what was before their eyes without quite knowing what they had rejected and why.

I felt that the Negro could not live a full, human life under the conditions imposed upon him by America; and I felt, too, that America, for different reasons, could not live a full, human life. It seemed to me, then, that if the Negro solved his problem, he would be solving infinitely more than his problem alone. I felt certain that the Negro could never solve his problem until the deeper problem of American civilization had been faced and solved. And because the Negro was the most cast-out of all the outcast people in America, I felt that no other group in America could tackle this problem of what our American lives meant so well as the Negro could.

But, as I listened to the Communist Negro speakers, I wondered if the Negro, blasted by three hundred years of oppression, could possibly cast off his fear and corruption and rise to the task. Could the Negro ever possess himself, learn to know what had happened to him in relation to the aspirations of Western society? It seemed to me that for the Negro to try to save himself he would have to forget himself and try to save a confused, materialistic nation from its own drift toward self-destruction. Could the Negro accomplish this miracle? Could he take up his bed and walk?

Election time was nearing and a Negro Republican precinct captain asked me to help him round up votes. I had no interest in the candidates, but I needed the money. I went from door to door with the precinct captain and discovered that the whole business was one long process of bribery, that people voted for three dollars, for the right to continue their illicit trade in sex or alcohol. On election day I went into the polling booth and drew the curtain behind me and unfolded my ballots. As I stood there the sordid implications of politics flashed through my mind. "Big Bill" Thompson headed the local Republican machine and I knew that he was using the Negro vote to control the city hall; in turn, he was engaged in vast political deals of which the Negro voters, political innocents, had no notion. With my pencil I wrote in a determined scrawl across the face of the ballots:

## I Protest This Fraud

I knew that my gesture was futile. But I wanted somebody to know that out of that vast sea of ignorance in the Black Belt there was at least one person who knew the game for what it was. I collected my ten dollars and went home.

The depression deepened and I could not sell insurance to hungry Negroes. I sold my watch and scouted for cheaper rooms; I found a rotting building and rented an apartment in it. The place was dismal; plaster was falling from the walls; the wooden stairs sagged. When my mother saw it, she wept. I felt bleak. I had not done what I had come to the city to do.

One morning I rose and my mother told me that there was no food for breakfast. I knew that the city had opened relief stations, but each time I thought of going into one of them I burned with shame. I sat four hours, fighting hunger, avoiding my mother's eyes. Then I rose, put on my hat and coat, and went out. As I walked toward the Cook County Bureau of Public Welfare to plead for bread, I knew that I had come to the end of something.

# Chapter III

W HEN I reached the relief station, I felt that I was making a public confession of my hunger. I sat waiting for hours, resentful of the mass of hungry people about me. My turn finally came and I was questioned by a middle-class Negro woman who asked me for a short history of my life. As I waited again I became aware of something happening in the room. The black men and women were mumbling quietly among themselves; they had not known one another before they had come here, but now their timidity and shame were wearing off and they were exchanging experiences. Before this they had lived as individuals, each somewhat afraid of the other, each seeking his own pleasure, each staunch in that degree of Americanism that had been allowed him. But now life had tossed them together, and they were learning to know the sentiments of their neighbors for the first time; their talking was enabling them to sense the collectivity of their lives, and some of their fear was passing.

Did the relief officials realize what was happening? No. If they had, they would have stopped it. But they saw their "clients" through the eyes of their profession, saw only what their "science" allowed them to see. As I listened to the talk I could see black minds shedding many illusions. These people now knew that the past had betrayed them, had cast them out; but they did not know what the future would be like, did not know what they wanted. Yes, some of the things that the Communists said were true; they maintained that there came times in history when a ruling class could no longer rule, and I sat looking at the beginnings of anarchy. To permit the birth of this new consciousness in these people was proof that those who ruled did not quite know what they were doing, assuming that they were trying to save themselves and their class. Had they understood what was happening, they would never have allowed millions of perplexed and defeated people to sit together for long hours and talk, for out of their talk was rising a new realization of life. And once this new conception of themselves had formed, no power on earth could alter it.

I left the relief station with the promise that food would be sent to me, but I also left with a knowledge that the relief officials had not wanted to give to me. I had felt the possibility of creating a new understanding of life in the minds of people rejected by the society in which they lived, people to whom the Chicago *Daily Tribune* referred contemptuously as the "idle" ones, as though these people had deliberately sought their present state of helplessness.

Who would give these people a meaningful way of life? Communist theory defined these people as the molders of the future of mankind, but the Communist speeches I had heard in the park had mocked that definition. These people, of course, were not ready for a revolution; they had not abandoned their past lives by choice, but because they simply could not live the old way any longer. Now, what new faith would they embrace? The day I begged bread from the city officials was the day that showed me I was not alone in my loneliness, society had cast millions of others with me. But how could I be with them? How many understood what was happening? My mind swam with questions that I could not answer.

I was slowly beginning to comprehend the meaning of my environment; a sense of direction was beginning to emerge from the conditions of my life. I began to feel something more powerful than I could express. My speech and manner changed. My cynicism slid from me. I grew open and questioning. I wanted to know.

(If I were a member of the class that rules, I would post men in all the neighborhoods of the nation, not to spy upon or club rebellious workers, not to break strikes or disrupt unions; but to ferret out those who no longer respond to the system in which they live. I would make it known that the real danger does not stem from those who seek to grab their share of wealth through force, or from those who try to defend their property through violence, for both of these groups, by their affirmative acts, support the values of the system in which they live. The millions that I would fear are those who do not dream of the prizes that the nation holds forth, for it is in them, though they may not know it, that a revolution has taken place and is biding its time to translate itself into a new and strange way of life.

(I feel that the Negroes' relation to America is symbolically peculiar, and from the Negroes' ultimate reactions to their trapped state a lesson can be learned about America's future. Negroes are told in a language they cannot possibly misunderstand that their native land is not their own; and when they, acting upon impulses which they share with whites, try to assert a claim to their birthright, whites retaliate with terror, never pausing to consider the consequences should the Negroes give up completely. They never dream that they would face a situation far more terrifying if they were confronted by Negroes who made no claims at all than by those who are buoyed by social aggressiveness. My knowledge of how Negroes react to their plight makes me declare that no man can possibly be individually guilty of treason, that an insurgent act is but a man's desperate answer to those who twist his environment so that he cannot fully share the spirit of his native land. Treason is a crime of the state.)

Christmas came and I was once more called to the post office for temporary work. Again I met the Irish chap and we discussed world happenings, the vast armies of unemployed, the rising tide of radical action. I now detected a change in the attitudes of the whites I met; their privations were making them regard Negroes with new eyes, and for the first time I was invited to their homes.

When the work in the post office ended, I was assigned by the relief system as an orderly to a medical research institute in one of the largest and wealthiest hospitals in Chicago. I cleaned operating rooms, dog, rat, mice, cat, and rabbit pens, and fed guinea pigs. Four of us Negroes worked there and we occupied an underworld position, remembering that we must restrict ourselves—when not engaged upon some task—to the basement corridors so that we would not mingle with white nurses, doctors, or visitors.

The sharp line of racial division drawn by the hospital authorities came to me the first morning when I walked along an underground corridor and saw two long lines of women coming toward me. A line of white girls marched past, clad in starched uniforms that gleamed white; their faces were alert, their steps quick, their bodies lean and shapely, their shoulders erect, their faces lit with the light of purpose. And after them came a line of black girls, old, fat, dressed in ragged gingham, walking loosely, carrying tin cans of soap powder, rags, mops, brooms . . . I wondered what law of the universe kept them from being mixed? The sun would not have stopped shining had there been a few black girls in the first line, and the earth would not have stopped whirling on its axis had there been a few white girls in the second line. But the two lines I saw graded status in purely racial terms.

Of the three Negroes who worked with me, one was a boy of about my own age, Bill, who was either sleepy or drunk most of the time. Bill straightened his hair and I suspected that he kept a bottle hidden somewhere in the piles of hay which we fed to

46

the guinea pigs. He did not like me and I did not like him, though I tried harder than he to conceal my dislike. We had nothing in common except that we were both black and lost. While I contained my frustration, he drank to drown his. Often I tried to talk to him, tried in simple words to convey to him some of my ideas, and he would listen in sullen silence. Then one day he came to me with an angry look on his face.

"I got it," he said.

"You've got what?" I asked.

"This old race problem you keep talking about," he said.

"What about it?"

"Well, it's this way," he explained seriously. "Let the government give every man a gun and five bullets, then let us all start over again. Make it just like it was in the beginning. The ones who come out on top, white or black, let them rule."

His simplicity terrified me. I had never met a Negro who was so irredeemably brutalized. I stopped pumping my ideas into Bill's brain for fear that the fumes of alcohol might send him reeling toward some fantastic fate.

The two other Negroes were elderly and had been employed in the institute for fifteen years or more. One was Brand, a short, black, morose bachelor; the other was Cooke, a tall, yellow, spectacled fellow who spent his spare time keeping track of world events through the Chicago *Daily Tribune.* Brand and Cooke hated each other for a reason that I was never able to determine, and they spent a good part of each day quarreling.

When I began working at the institute, I recalled my adolescent dream of wanting to be a medical research worker. Daily I saw young Jewish boys and girls receiving instruction in chemistry and medicine that the average black boy or girl could never receive. When I was alone, I wandered and poked my fingers into strange chemicals, watched intricate machines trace red and black lines upon ruled paper. At times I paused and stared at the walls of the rooms, at the floors, at the wide desks at which the white doctors sat; and I realized—with a feeling that I could never quite get used to—that I was looking at the world of another race.

My interest in what was happening in the institute amused the three other Negroes with whom I worked. They had no curiosity about "white folks' things," while I wanted to know if the dogs being treated for diabetes were getting well; if the rats and mice in whom cancer had been induced showed any signs of responding to treatment. I wanted to know the principle that lay behind the Aschheim-Zondek tests that were made with rabbits, the Wassermann tests that were made with guinea pigs. But when I asked a timid question I found that even Jewish doctors had learned to imitate the sadistic method of humbling a Negro that the native-born whites had cultivated.

"If you know too much, boy, your brains might explode," a doctor said one day.

Each Saturday morning I assisted a young Jewish doctor in slitting the vocal cords of a fresh batch of dogs from the city pound. The object was to devocalize the dogs so that their howls would not disturb the patients in the other parts of the hospital. I held each dog as the doctor injected nembutal into its veins to make it unconscious; then I held the dog's jaws open as the doctor inserted the scalpel and severed the vocal cords. Later, when the dogs came to, they would lift their heads to the ceiling and gape in a soundless wail. The sight became lodged in my imagination as a symbol of silent suffering.

To me nembutal was a powerful and mysterious liquid, but when I asked questions about its properties I could not obtain a single intelligent answer. The young Jewish doctor simply ignored me with:

"Come on. Bring the next dog. I haven't got all day."

One Saturday morning, after I had held the dogs for their vocal cords to be slit, the doctor left the nembutal on a bench. I picked it up, uncorked it, and smelt it. It was odorless. Suddenly Brand ran to me with a stricken face.

"What're you doing?" he asked.

"I was smelling this stuff to see if it had any odor," I said.

"Did you really smell it?" he asked me.

"Yes."

"Oh, God!" he exclaimed.

"What's the matter?" I asked.

"You shouldn't've done that!" he shouted.

"Why?"

He grabbed my arm and jerked me across the room.

"Come on!" he yelled, snatching open the door.

"What's the matter?" I asked.

"I gotta get you to a doctor 'fore it's too late," he gasped.

Had my foolish curiosity made me inhale something dangerous?

"But . . . Is it poisonous?"

"Run, boy!" he said, pulling me. "You'll fall dead."

Filled with fear, with Brand pulling my arm, I rushed out of the room, raced across a rear areaway, into another room, then down a long corridor. I wanted to ask Brand what symptoms I must expect, but we were running too fast. Brand finally stopped, gasping for breath. My heart beat wildly and my blood pounded in my head. Brand then dropped to the concrete floor, stretched out on his back and yelled with laughter, shaking all over. He beat his fists against the concrete; he moaned, giggled.

I tried to master my outrage, wondering if some of the white doctors had told him to play the joke. He rose and wiped tears from his eyes, still laughing. I walked away from him. He knew that I was angry and he followed me.

"Don't get mad," he gasped through his laughter.

"Go to hell," I said.

"I couldn't help it," he giggled. "You looked at me like you'd

49

believe anything I said. Man, you was scared . . ."

He leaned against the wall, laughing again, stomping his feet. I was angry, for I felt that he would spread the story. I knew that Bill and Cooke never ventured beyond the safe bounds of Negro living, and they would never blunder into anything like this. And if they heard about this, they would laugh for months.

"Brand, if you mention this, I'll kill you," I swore.

"You ain't mad?" he asked, laughing, staring at me through tears.

Sniffing, Brand walked ahead of me. I followed him back into the room that housed the dogs. All day, while at some task, he would pause and giggle, then smother it with his hand, looking at me out of the corner of his eyes, shaking his head. He laughed at me for a week. I kept my temper and let him amuse himself. I finally found out the properties of nembutal by consulting medical books, but I never told Brand.

One summer morning, just as I began work, a young Jewish boy came to me with a stop watch in his hand.

"Dr.—— wants me to time you when you clean a room," he said. "We're trying to make the institute more efficient."

"I'm doing my work and getting through on time," I said.

"This is the boss's order," he said.

"Why don't you work for a change?" I blurted, angry.

"Now, look," he said. "*This* is my work. Now *you* work."

I got a mop and pail, sprayed a room with disinfectant, and scrubbed at coagulated blood and hardened dog, rat, and rabbit feces. The normal temperature of a room was ninety, but as the sun beat down upon the skylights, the temperature rose above a hundred. Stripped to my waist, I slung the mop, moving steadily like a machine, hearing the Jewish boy press the button on the stop watch as I finished cleaning a room. I worked from seven in the morning until noon, and I was limp, washed-out.

"Well, how is it?" I asked.

"It took you seventeen minutes to clean that last room," he said. "That ought to be the time for each room."

"But that room was not very dirty," I said.

"You have seventeen rooms to clean," he went on as though I had not spoken. "Seventeen times seventeen makes four hours and forty-nine minutes." He wrote upon a little pad. "After lunch, clean the five flights of stone stairs. I timed a boy who scrubbed one step and multiplied that time by the number of steps. You ought to be through at six."

"Suppose I want relief?" I asked.

"You'll manage," he said and left.

Never had I felt so much the slave as when I scoured those stone steps each afternoon. Working against time, I would wet five steps, sprinkle soap powder, then a white doctor or a nurse would come and, instead of avoiding the soppy steps, walk on them and track the dirty water onto the steps that I had already cleaned. To obviate this, I cleaned but two steps at a time, a distance over which a ten-year-old child could step. But it did no good. The white people still plopped their feet down into the dirty water and muddied the other clean steps. If I ever really hotly hated unthinking whites, it was then. Not once during my entire stay at the institute did a single white person show enough courtesy to avoid a wet step. I would be on my knees, scrubbing, sweating, pouring out what limited energy my body could wring from my meager diet, and I would hear feet approaching. I would pause and curse with tense lips:

"These sonofabitches are going to dirty these steps again, goddamn their souls to hell!"

Sometimes a sadistically observant white man would notice that he had tracked dirty water up the steps, and he would look back down at me and smile and say:

"Boy, we sure keep you busy, don't we?"

51

And I would not be able to answer.

The feud that went on between Brand and Cooke continued. Although they were working daily in a building where scientific history was being made, the light of curiosity was never in their eyes. They were conditioned to their racial "place," had learned to see only a part of the whites and the white world; and the whites, too, had learned to see only a part of the lives of the blacks and their world.

Perhaps Brand and Cooke, lacking interests that could absorb them, fuming like children over trifles, simply invented their hate of each other in order to have something to feel deeply about. Or perhaps there was in them a vague psyche pain stemming from their chronically frustrating way of life, a pain whose cause they did not know; and, like those devocalized dogs, they would whirl and snap at the air when their old pain struck them. Anyway, they argued about the weather, sports, sex, war, race, politics, and religion; neither of them knew the subjects they debated, but it seemed that the less they knew the better they could argue.

The tug of war between the two elderly men reached a climax one winter day at noon. It was incredibly cold and an icy gale swept up and down the Chicago streets with blizzard force. The door of the animal-filled room was locked, for we always insisted that we be allowed one hour in which to eat and rest. Bill and I were sitting on wooden boxes, eating our lunches out of paper bags. Brand was washing his hands at the sink. Cooke was sitting on a rickety stool, munching an apple and reading the Chicago *Daily Tribune.*

Now and then a devocalized dog lifted his nose to the ceiling and howled soundlessly. The room was filled with many rows of high steel tiers. Perched upon each of these tiers were layers of steel cages containing the dogs, rats, mice, rabbits, and guinea pigs. Each cage was labeled in some indecipherable scientific jargon. Along the walls of the room were long charts with zigzagging red and black lines that traced the success or failure of some experiment. The lonely piping of guinea pigs floated unheeded about us. Hay rustled as a rabbit leaped restlessly about in its pen. A rat scampered around in its steel prison. Cooke tapped the newspaper for attention.

"It says here," Cooke mumbled through a mouthful of apple, "that this is the coldest day since 1888."

Bill and I sat unconcerned. Brand chuckled softly.

"What in hell you laughing about?" Cooke demanded of Brand.

"You can't believe what that damn *Tribune* says," Brand said.

"How come I can't?" Cooke demanded. "It's the world's greatest newspaper."

Brand did not reply; he shook his head pityingly and chuckled again.

"Stop that damn laughing at me!" Cooke said angrily.

"I laugh as much as I wanna," Brand said. "You don't know what you talking about. The *Herald-Examiner* says it's the coldest day since 1873."

"But the *Trib* oughta know," Cooke countered. "It's older'n that *Examiner.*"

"That damn *Trib* don't know nothing!" Brand drowned out Cooke's voice.

"How in hell you know?" Cooke asked with rising anger.

The argument waxed until Cooke shouted that if Brand did not shut up he was going to cut his "black throat."

Brand whirled from the sink, his hands dripping soapy water, his eyes blazing.

"Take that back," Brand said.

"I take nothing back! What you wanna do about it?" Cooke taunted.

The two elderly Negroes glared at each other. I wondered if the quarrel was really serious, or if it would turn out harmlessly as so many others had done.

Suddenly Cooke dropped the Chicago *Daily Tribune* and

pulled a long knife from his pocket; his thumb pressed a button and a gleaming steel blade leaped out. Brand stepped back quickly and seized an ice pick that was stuck in a wooden board above the sink.

"Put that knife down," Brand said.

"Stay 'way from me, or I'll cut your throat," Cooke warned.

Brand lunged with the ice pick. Cooke dodged out of range. They circled each other like fighters in a prize ring. The cancerous and tubercular rats and mice leaped about their cages. The guinea pigs whistled in fright. The diabetic dogs bared their teeth and barked soundlessly in our direction. The Aschheim-Zondek rabbits flopped their ears and tried to hide in the corners of their pens. Cooke now crouched and sprang forward with the knife. Bill and I jumped to our feet, speechless with surprise. Brand retreated. The eyes of both men were hard and unblinking; they were breathing deeply.

"Say, cut it out!" I called in alarm.

"Them damn fools is really fighting," Bill said in amazement.

Slashing at each other, Brand and Cooke surged up and down the aisles of steel tiers. Suddenly Brand uttered a bellow and charged into Cooke and swept him violently backward. Cooke grasped Brand's hand to keep the ice pick from sinking into his chest. Brand broke free and charged Cooke again, sweeping him into an animal-filled steel tier. The tier balanced itself on its edge for an indecisive moment, then toppled.

Like kingpins, one steel tier lammed into another, then they all crashed to the floor with a sound as of the roof falling. The whole aspect of the room altered quicker than the eye could follow. Brand and Cooke stood stock-still, their eyes fastened upon each other, their pointed weapons raised; but they were dimly aware of the havoc that churned about them.

The steel tiers lay jumbled; the doors of the cages swung open. Rats and mice and dogs and rabbits moved over the floor in wild panic. The Wassermann guinea pigs were squealing as though judgment day had come. Here and there an animal had been crushed beneath a cage.

All four of us looked at one another. We knew what this meant. We might lose our jobs. We were already regarded as black dunces, and if the doctors saw this mess they would take it as final proof. Bill rushed to the door to make sure that it was locked. I glanced at the clock and saw that it was 12:30. We had one half hour of grace.

"Come on," Bill said uneasily. "We got to get this place cleaned."

Brand and Cooke stared at each other, both doubting.

"Give me your knife, Cooke," I said.

"Naw! Take Brand's ice pick *first,*" Cooke said.

"The hell you say!" Brand said. "Take his knife *first!*"

A knock sounded at the door.

"Sssshh," Bill said.

We waited. We heard footsteps going away. We'll all lose our jobs, I thought.

Persuading the fighters to surrender their weapons was a difficult task, but at last it was done and we could begin to right things. Slowly Brand stooped and tugged at one end of a steel tier. Cooke stooped to help him. Both men seemed to be acting in a dream. Soon, however, all four of us were working frantically, watching the clock.

As we labored we conspired to keep the fight a secret; we agreed to tell the doctors—if any should ask—that we had not been in the room during our lunch hour; we felt that that lie would explain why no one had unlocked the door when the knock had come.

We righted the tiers and replaced the cages; then we were faced with the impossible task of sorting the cancerous rats and mice, the diabetic dogs, the Aschheim-Zondek rabbits, and the

Wassermann guinea pigs. Whether we kept our jobs or not depended upon how shrewdly we could cover up all evidence of the fight. It was pure guesswork, but we had to try to put the animals back into the correct cages. We knew that certain rats or mice went into certain cages, but we did not know *what* rat or mouse went into *what* cage. We did not know a tubercular mouse from a cancerous mouse; the white doctors had made sure that we would not know. They had never taken time to answer a single question; though we worked in the institute, we were as remote from the meaning of the experiments as if we lived in the moon. The doctors had laughed at what they felt was our childlike interest in the fate of the animals.

First we sorted the dogs; that was fairly easy, for we could remember the size and color of most of them. But the rats and mice and guinea pigs baffled us completely.

We put our heads together and pondered, down in the underworld of the great scientific institute. It was a strange scientific conference; the fate of the entire medical research institute rested in our ignorant, black hands.

We remembered the number of rats, mice, or guinea pigs—we had to handle them several times each day—that went into a given cage, and we supplied the number helter-skelter from those animals that we could catch running loose on the floor. We discovered that many rats, mice, and guinea pigs were missing; they had been killed in the scuffle. We solved that problem by taking healthy stock from other cages and putting them into cages with sick animals. We repeated this process until we were certain that, numerically at least, all the animals with which the doctors were experimenting were accounted for.

The rabbits came last. We broke the rabbits down into two general groups: those that had fur on their bellies and those that did not. We knew that all those rabbits that had shaven bellies —our scientific knowledge adequately covered this point because it was our job to shave the rabbits—were undergoing Aschheim-Zondek tests. But in what pen did a given rabbit belong? We did not know. I solved the problem very simply. I counted the shaven rabbits; they numbered seventeen. I counted the pens labeled "Aschheim-Zondek," then proceeded to drop a shaven rabbit into each pen at random. And again we were numerically successful. At least white America had taught us how to count . . .

Lastly we carefully wrapped all the dead animals in newspapers and hid their bodies in a garbage can.

At a few minutes to one the room was in order; that is, the kind of order that we four Negroes could figure out. I unlocked the door and we sat waiting, whispering, vowing secrecy, wondering what the reaction of the doctors would be.

Finally a doctor came, gray-haired, white-coated, spectacled, efficient, serious, taciturn, bearing a tray upon which sat a bottle of mysterious fluid and a hypodermic needle.

"My rats, please."

Cooke shuffled forward to serve him. We held our breath. Cooke got the cage which he knew the doctor always called for at that hour and brought it forward. One by one, Cooke took out the rats and held them as the doctor solemnly injected the mysterious fluid under their skins.

"Thank you, Cooke," the doctor murmured.

"Not at all, sir," Cooke mumbled with a suppressed gasp.

When the doctor had gone we looked at one another, hardly daring to believe that our secret would be kept. We were so anxious that we did not know whether to curse or laugh. Another doctor came.

"Give me A-Z rabbit number 14."

"Yes, sir," I said.

I brought him the rabbit and he took it upstairs to the operating room. We waited for repercussions. None came.

All that afternoon the doctors came and went. I would run into the room—stealing a few seconds from my step scrubbing—and ask what progress was being made and would learn that the doctors had detected nothing. At quitting time we felt triumphant.

"They won't never know," Cooke boasted in a whisper.

I saw Brand stiffen. I knew that he was aching to dispute Cooke's optimism, but the memory of the fight he had just had was so fresh in his mind that he could not speak.

Another day went by and nothing happened. Then another day. The doctors examined the animals and wrote in their little black books, in their big black books, and continued to trace red and black lines upon the charts.

A week passed and we felt out of danger. Not one question had been asked.

Of course, we four black men were much too modest to make our contribution known, but we often wondered what went on in the laboratories after that secret disaster. Was some scientific hypothesis, well on its way to validation and ultimate public use, discarded because of unexpected findings on that cold winter day? Was some tested principle given a new and strange refinement because of fresh, remarkable evidence? Did some brooding research worker—those who held stop watches and slopped their feet carelessly in the water of the steps I tried so hard to keep clean—get a wild, if brief, glimpse of a new scientific truth? Well, we never heard . . .

I brooded, of course, upon whether I should have gone to the director's office and told him what had happened, but each time I thought of it I remembered that the director had been the man who had ordered the boy to stand over me while I was working and time my movements with a stop watch. He did not regard me as a human being. I did not share his world. I earned thirteen dollars a week and I had to support four people with it, and should I risk that thirteen dollars by acting idealistically? Brand and

Cooke would have hated me and would have eventually driven me from the job had I "told" on them. The hospital kept us four Negroes, as though we were close kin to the animals we tended, huddled together down in the underworld corridors of the hospital, separated by a vast psychological distance from the significant processes of the rest of the hospital—just as America had kept us locked in the dark underworld of American life for three hundred years—and we had made our own code of ethics, values, loyalty.

# Chapter IV

ONE Thursday night I received an invitation from a group of white boys I had known in the post office to meet in a South Side hotel and argue the state of the world. About ten of us gathered and ate salami sandwiches, drank beer, and talked. I was amazed to discover that many of them had joined the Communist party. I challenged them by reciting the antics of the Negro Communists I had seen in the parks, and I was told that those antics were "tactics" and were all right. I was dubious.

Then one Thursday night Sol, a Jewish chap, startled us by announcing that he had had a short story accepted by a little magazine called the *Anvil*, edited by Jack Conroy, and that he had joined a revolutionary artists' organization, the John Reed Club. Sol repeatedly begged me to attend the meetings of the club, but I always found an easy excuse for refusing.

"You'd like them," Sol said.

"I don't want to be organized," I said.

"They can help you to write," he said.

"Nobody can tell me how or what to write," I said.

"Come and see," he urged. "What have you to lose?"

I felt that Communists could not possibly have a sincere interest in Negroes. I was cynical and I would rather have heard a white man say that he hated Negroes, which I could have readily believed, than to have heard him say that he respected Negroes, which would have made me doubt him. I did not think that there existed many whites who, through intellectual effort, could lift themselves out of the traditions of their times and see the Negro objectively.

One Saturday night, sitting home idle, not caring to visit the girls I had met on my former insurance route, bored with reading, I decided to appear at the John Reed Club in the capacity of an amused spectator. I rode to the Loop and found the number. A dark stairway led upwards; it did not look welcoming. What on earth of importance could transpire in so dingy a place? Through the windows above me I saw vague murals along the walls. I mounted the stairs to a door that was lettered:

### The Chicago John Reed Club

I opened it and stepped into the strangest room I had ever seen. Paper and cigarette butts lay on the floor. A few benches ran along the walls, above which were vivid colors depicting colossal figures of workers carrying streaming banners. The mouths of the workers gaped in wild cries; their legs were sprawled over cities.

"Hello."

I turned and saw a white man smiling at me.

"A friend of mine, who's a member of this club, asked me to visit here. His name is Sol ——," I told him.

"You're welcome here," the white man said. "We're not having an affair tonight. We're holding an editorial meeting. Do you paint?" He was slightly gray and he had a mustache.

"No," I said. "I try to write."

"Then sit in on the editorial meeting of our magazine, *Left Front,*" he suggested.

"I know nothing of editing," I said.

"You can learn," he said.

I stared at him, doubting.

"I don't want to be in the way here," I said.

"My name's Grimm," he said.

61

I told him my name and we shook hands. He went to a closet and returned with an armful of magazines.

"Here are some back issues of the *Masses,*" he said. "Have you ever read it?"

"No," I said.

"Some of the best writers in America publish in it," he explained. He also gave me copies of a magazine called *International Literature.* "There's stuff here from Gide, Gorky . . ."

I assured him that I would read them. He took me to an office and introduced me to a Jewish boy who was to become one of the nation's leading painters, to a chap who was to become one of the eminent composers of his day, to a writer who was to create some of the best novels of his generation, to a young Jewish boy who was destined to film the Nazi invasion of Czechoslovakia. I was meeting men and women whom I would know for decades to come, who were to form the first sustained relationships in my life.

I sat in a corner and listened while they discussed their magazine, *Left Front.* Were they treating me courteously because I was a Negro? I must let cold reason guide me with these people, I told myself. I was asked to contribute something to the magazine, and I said vaguely that I would consider it. After the meeting I met an Irish girl who worked for an advertising agency, a girl who did social work, a schoolteacher, and the wife of a prominent university professor. I had once worked as a servant for people like these and I was skeptical. I tried to fathom their motives, but I could detect no condescension in them.

I went home full of reflection, probing the sincerity of the strange white people I had met, wondering how they *really* regarded Negroes. I lay on my bed and read the magazines and was amazed to find that there did exist in this world an organized search for the truth of the lives of the oppressed and the isolated. When I had begged bread from the officials, I had wondered dimly if the outcasts could become united in action, thought, and feeling. Now I knew. It was being done in one-sixth of the earth already. The revolutionary words leaped from the printed page and struck me with tremendous force.

It was not the economics of Communism, nor the great power of trade unions, nor the excitement of underground politics that claimed me; my attention was caught by the similarity of the experiences of workers in other lands, by the possibility of uniting scattered but kindred peoples into a whole. My cynicism—which had been my protection against an America that had cast me out —slid from me and, timidly, I began to wonder if a solution of unity was possible. My life as a Negro in America had led me to feel—though my helplessness had made me try to hide it from myself—that the problem of human unity was more important than bread, more important than physical living itself; for I felt that without a common bond uniting men, without a continuous current of shared thought and feeling circulating through the social system, like blood coursing through the body, there could be no living worthy of being called human.

I hungered to share the dominant assumptions of my time and act upon them. I did not want to feel, like an animal in a jungle, that the whole world was alien and hostile. I did not want to make individual war or individual peace. So far I had managed to keep humanly alive through transfusions from books. In my concrete relations with others I had encountered nothing to encourage me to believe in my feelings. It had been by denying what I saw with my eyes, disputing what I felt with my body, that I had managed to keep my identity intact. But it seemed to me that here at last in the realm of revolutionary expression was where Negro experience could find a home, a functioning value and role. Out of the magazines I read came a passionate call for the experiences of the disinherited, and there were none of the same lispings of the missionary in it. It did not say: "Be like us and we will like you,

63

maybe." It said: "If you possess enough courage to speak out what you are, you will find that you are not alone." It urged life to believe in life.

I read on into the night; then, toward dawn, I swung from bed and inserted paper into the typewriter. Feeling for the first time that I could speak to listening ears, I wrote a wild, crude poem in free verse, coining images of black hands playing, working, holding bayonets, stiffening finally in death . . . I read it and felt that in a clumsy way it linked white life with black, merged two streams of common experience.

I heard someone poking about the kitchen.

"Richard, are you ill?" my mother called.

"No. I'm reading."

My mother opened the door and stared curiously at the pile of magazines that lay upon my pillow.

"You're not throwing away money buying those magazines, are you?" she asked.

"No. They were given to me."

She hobbled to the bed on her crippled legs and picked up a copy of the *Masses* that carried a lurid May Day cartoon. She adjusted her glasses and peered at it for a long time.

"My God in heaven," she breathed in horror.

"What's the matter, mama?"

"What is this?" she asked, extending the magazine to me, pointing to the cover. "What's wrong with that man?"

With my mother standing at my side, lending me her eyes, I stared at a cartoon drawn by a Communist artist; it was the figure of a worker clad in ragged overalls and holding aloft a red banner. The man's eyes bulged; his mouth gaped as wide as his face; his teeth showed; the muscles of his neck were like ropes. Following the man was a horde of nondescript men, women, and children, waving clubs, stones, and pitchforks.

"What are those people going to do?" my mother asked.

"I don't know," I hedged.

"Are these Communist magazines?"

"Yes."

"And do they want people to act like this?"

"Well . . ." I hesitated.

My mother's face showed disgust and moral loathing. She was a gentle woman. Her ideal was Christ upon the cross. How could I tell her that the Communist party wanted her to march in the streets, chanting, singing?

"What do Communists think people are?" she asked.

"They don't quite mean what you see there," I said, fumbling with my words.

"Then what do they mean?"

"This is symbolic," I said.

"Then why don't they speak out what they mean?"

"Maybe they don't know how."

"Then why do they print this stuff?"

"They don't quite know how to appeal to people yet," I admitted, wondering whom I could convince of this if I could not convince my mother.

"That picture's enough to drive a body crazy," she said, dropping the magazine, turning to leave, then pausing at the door. "You're not getting mixed up with those people?"

"I'm just reading, mama," I dodged.

My mother left and I brooded upon the fact that I had not been able to meet her simple challenge. I looked again at the cover of the *Masses* and I knew that the wild cartoon did not reflect the passions of the common people. I reread the magazine and was convinced that much of the expression embodied what the *artists* thought would appeal to others, what they thought would gain recruits. They had a program, an ideal, but they had not yet found a language.

Here, then, was something that I could do, reveal, say. The

65

Communists, I felt, had oversimplified the experience of those whom they sought to lead. In their efforts to recruit masses, they had missed the meaning of the lives of the masses, had conceived of people in too abstract a manner. I would make voyages, discoveries, explorations with words and try to put some of that meaning back. I would address my words to two groups: I would tell Communists how common people felt, and I would tell common people of the self-sacrifice of Communists who strove for unity among them.

That following Thursday night, when I joined my friends at the hotel for beer, I pulled out my crude verses and laid them on the table. Sol read them.

"This can be published," he said.

"That's not the point," I said. "What do they mean to you?"

"This is the vision of the disinherited," he said.

"If you're going to publish these to recruit me into the party, then nothing doing," I said.

"They'll be published whether you join or not," he said.

I told the group of my mother's reaction to the *Masses* cartoon.

"She'll have to learn the symbolism of the revolution," somebody said.

"But why can't Communism speak a language she understands?" I asked.

There was a lot of argument that went nowhere.

Still suspicious, my eyes watching for the slightest anti-Negro gesture, I attended the next meeting of the club. In the end I had to admit that they were glad to have me with them. But I still doubted their motives. Were they trying to get my head bashed in a picket line so that they could capitalize on the publicity? Or did the discipline of the club demand that they be friendly with me? If that was true, then those who did not want a Negro in the club could resign. But no one made a move to resign. How had these people, denying profit and home and God, made that hurdle that even the churches of America had not been able to make?

The editor of *Left Front* accepted two of my crude poems for publication, sent two of them to Jack Conroy's *Anvil*, and sent another to the *New Masses*, the successor of the *Masses*. Doubts still lingered in my mind.

"Don't send them if you think they're aren't good enough," I said.

"They're good enough," he said.

"Are you doing this to get me to join up?" I asked.

"No," he said. "Your poems are crude, but good for us. You see, we're all new in this. We write articles about Negroes, but we never see any Negroes. We need your stuff."

I sat through several meetings of the club and was impressed by the scope and seriousness of its activities. The club was demanding that the government create jobs for unemployed artists; it planned and organized art exhibits; it raised funds for the publication of *Left Front;* and it sent scores of speakers to trade-union meetings. The members were fervent, democratic, restless, eager, self-sacrificing. I was convinced, and my response was to set myself the task of making Negroes know what Communists were. While mopping the operating rooms of the medical research institute, I got the notion of writing a series of biographical sketches of Negro Communists. I told no one of my intentions, and I did not know how fantastically naïve my ambition was.

I had attended but a few meetings before I realized that a bitter factional fight was in progress between two groups of members of the club. But when I tried to learn the nature of the fight, no one would tell me anything. Sharp arguments rose at every meeting. I noticed that a small group of painters actually led the club and dominated its policies. The group of writers that centered about *Left Front* resented the leadership of the painters. Being primarily interested in *Left Front,* I sided in simple loyalty with the writers. Then came a strange development. The *Left Front* group declared that the incumbent leadership did not reflect the wishes of the club. A special meeting was called and a motion was made to reelect an executive secretary. When nominations were made for the office, my name was included. I declined the nomination, telling the members that I was too ignorant of their aims to be seriously considered. The debate lasted all night. A vote was taken in the early hours of morning by a show of hands, and I was elected. I had been a member of the club for less than two months and did not fully understand the purposes of the organization.

Later I learned what had happened: the writers of the club had decided to "use" me to oust the painters, who were party members, from the leadership of the club. Without my knowledge and consent, they confronted the members of the party with a Negro, knowing that it would be difficult for Communists to refuse to vote for a man representing the largest single racial minority in the nation, inasmuch as Negro equality was one of the main tenets of Communism.

Though I was not a Communist, cynical rivalry had put me in charge of one of the party's leading cultural organizations. At once I offered my resignation, but the members would not hear of it. I could not determine if they were acting sincerely. I was afraid that the defeated secretary, being white, would resent losing to a Negro, but his conduct showed nothing but friendliness.

As the club's leader, I soon learned the nature of the fight. The Communists had secretly organized a "fraction" in the club; that is, a small portion of the club's members were secret members of the Communist party. They would meet outside of the club, decide what policies the club should follow; and when they put forth their proposals in open meetings, the sheer strength of their arguments usually persuaded nonparty members to vote with them. The crux of the fight was that the nonparty members resented the excessive demands made upon the club by the local

party authorities through the fraction. For example, the fraction demanded that the *Daily Worker* and the *New Masses,* official periodicals of the Communist party, be put on sale at all meetings. The nonparty group declared that this would limit the club's membership to those who already believed in Communism.

The demands of the local party authorities for money, speakers, and poster painters were so great that the publication of *Left Front* was in danger. Many young writers had joined the club because of their hope of publishing in *Left Front,* and when the Communist party sent word through the fraction that the magazine should be dissolved, the writers rejected the decision, an act which was interpreted as hostility toward party authority.

I pleaded with the party members for a more liberal program for the club. Feelings waxed violent and bitter. Then the showdown came. I was informed that if I wanted to continue as secretary of the club I would have to join the Communist party. I stated that I favored a policy that allowed for the development of writers and artists. My policy was accepted. I signed the membership card.

As the club's leader, I strove to keep the quarrels within limits by striking a series of compromises: for example, the sale of the *Daily Worker* was withdrawn, but the sale of the *New Masses* was continued. My position was in the "middle"; the fraction urged me to collect money from the members for the Communist party, and the members urged me to fight for the continuance of *Left Front,* which had been branded as "useless" by the Communist party. Trying to please everybody, I pleased nobody. The club's energies were sapped by internal strife. Bills piled up. Rent fell past due. I wanted the club to continue at all hazards; my feelings were intensely personal. The club was my first contact with the modern world. I had lived so utterly isolated a life that the club filled for me a need that could not be imagined by the white members who were becoming disgusted with it, whose normal

living had given them what I was so desperately trying to get.

One night a Jewish chap appeared at one of our meetings and introduced himself as Comrade Young of Detroit. He told us that he was a member of the Communist party, a member of the Detroit John Reed Club, that he planned to make his home in Chicago. He was a short, friendly, black-haired, well-read fellow with hanging lips and bulging eyes. Shy of forces to execute the demands of the Communist party, we welcomed him. But I could not make out Young's personality; whenever I asked him a simple question, he looked off and stammered a confused answer. I decided to send his references to the Communist party for checking and forthwith named him for membership in the club. He's okay, I thought. Just a queer artist . . .

After the meeting Comrade Young confronted me with a problem. He had no money, he said, and asked if he could sleep temporarily on the club's premises. Believing him loyal, I gave him permission. Straightway Young became one of the most ardent members of our organization, admired by all. His paintings —which I did not understand—impressed our best artists. No report about Young had come from the Communist party, but since Young seemed a conscientious worker, I did not think the omission serious in any case.

At a meeting one night Young asked that his name be placed upon the agenda; when his time came to speak, he rose and launched into one of the most violent and bitter political attacks upon Swann, one of our best young artists, in the club's history. We were aghast. Young accused Swann of being a traitor to the workers, an opportunist, a collaborator with the police, and an adherent of Trotsky. Naturally most of the club's members assumed that Young, a member of the party, was voicing the ideas of the party. Surprised and baffled, I moved that Young's statement be referred to the executive committee for decision. Swann rightfully protested; he declared that he had been attacked in public and would answer in public.

It was voted that Swann should have the floor. He refuted Young's wild charges, but the majority of the club's members were bewildered, did not know whether to believe him or not. We all liked Swann, did not believe him guilty of any misconduct; but we did not want to offend the party. A verbal battle ensued. Finally the members who had been silent in deference to the party rose and demanded of me that the foolish charges against Swann be withdrawn. Again I moved that the matter be referred to the executive committee, and again my proposal was voted down. The membership had now begun to distrust the party's motives. They were afraid to let an executive committee, the majority of whom were party members, pass upon the charges made by party member Young.

Three meetings were consumed in bitter debate. Between meetings we urged Young to tell us who had given him the authority to castigate Swann, and Young hinted darkly that he was acting under the orders of either the Central Committee of the Communist party or the Communist International. And we were naturally impressed. Who were we to question the decisions of political bodies so highly placed? I sympathized with Swann, but was afraid to say a word in his behalf for fear that I, too, would be charged.

A delegation of members asked me if I had anything to do with Young's charges. I was so hurt and humiliated that I disavowed all relations with Young. Determined to end the farce, I cornered Young and demanded to know who had given him authority.

"I've been asked to rid the club of traitors," he said.

"But Swann isn't a traitor," I said.

"We must have a purge," he said, his eyes bulging, his face quivering with passion.

I admitted his great revolutionary fervor, but I felt that his zeal was a trifle excessive. The situation became worse. A delegation of members informed me that if the charges against Swann were not withdrawn, they would resign in a body. I was frantic. I wrote to the Communist party to ask why orders had been issued to punish Swann, and a reply came back that no such orders had been issued. Then what was Young up to? Who was prompting him? I finally begged the club to let me place the matter before the leaders of the Communist party for decision. After a violent debate, my proposal was accepted.

One night ten of us met in an office of a leader of the party to hear Young restate his charges against Swann. The party leader, aloof and amused, gave Young the signal to begin. Young unrolled a sheaf of papers and declaimed a list of political charges that excelled in viciousness his previous charges. An instinct warned me that something was wrong, but I could not make out what it was. I stared at Young, feeling that he was making a dreadful mistake, but fearing him because he had, by his own account, the sanction of high political authority. When Young had finished the party leader asked:

"Will you allow me to read these charges?"

"Of course," said Young, surrendering a copy of his indictment. "You may keep that copy. I have ten carbons."

"Why did you make so many carbons?" the leader asked.

"I didn't want anyone to steal them," Young said.

"If this man's charges against me are taken seriously," Swann said, "I'll resign and publicly denounce the club."

"You see!" Young yelled. "He's with the police!"

I was sick. The meeting ended with a promise from the party leader to read the charges carefully and render a verdict as to whether Swann should be placed on trial or not. I was convinced that something was wrong, but I could not figure it out. One afternoon I went to the club to have a long talk with Young; but when I arrived, he was not there. Nor was he there the next day. For a week I sought Young in vain. What had become of the man? I asked about him far and wide, but could get no word. Meanwhile the club's members asked his whereabouts and they would not believe me when I told them that I did not know. Was he ill? Had he been picked up by the police?

Somebody suggested that we search Young's luggage which was still in the club's back room. One afternoon Comrade Grimm and I sneaked into the club's headquarters and opened Young's luggage. What we saw amazed and puzzled us. First of all, there was a scroll of paper twenty yards long—one page pasted to another —which had drawings depicting the history of the human race from a Marxist point of view. The first page was titled:

## A Pictorial Record of Man's Economic Progress

"This is terribly ambitious," I said.

"He's very studious," Grimm said.

There were long dissertations written in longhand; some were political and others dealt with the history of art. Finally we found a letter with a Detroit return address and I promptly wrote asking news of our esteemed member. A few days later a letter came which said in part:

Dear Sir:

In reply to your letter of the ———, we beg to inform you that Mr. Young, who was a patient in our institution and who escaped from our custody a few months ago, has been apprehended and returned to this institution for mental treatment.

I was thunderstruck. Was this true? Undoubtedly it was. Then what kind of club did we run that a lunatic could step into it and help run it? Were we all so mad that we could not detect a madman when we saw one? I called a meeting of a few of the most trusted members of the club and laid the matter before them. They were dumfounded. We swore ourselves to secrecy and decided to suppress the matter. We agreed that we had made a terrible mistake.

But, of course, we had no power to restrain the other members from asking questions. Swann hammered at us from meeting to meeting.

"Where is Comrade Young? Is he sick? Is he dead? Is he in jail? Did the Communist party order him to stay away from the club?"

And to these questions I could but lie:

"I've had no word from Comrade Young. As soon as any is received, I'll inform the club."

Meanwhile I made a motion that all charges against Swann be dropped, which was done. I offered Swann an apology but, as the leader of the Chicago John Reed Club, I was a completely sober and chastened Communist.

# Chapter V

I HAD read widely in revolutionary literature, had observed many Communists, white and black, and had learned to know the daily hazards they faced and the sacrifices they made. I now wanted to give time to writing the book of biographical sketches I had planned. I did not know Negro Communists as well as I wanted to, and when, on many occasions, I had sought to question them about their feelings, their work, and their actions, they had been reticent. My zeal made me forget these rebuffs, for I was sure that an atmosphere of trust would be created as soon as I had explained my project to them.

The Communist party fraction in the John Reed Club instructed me to ask my party cell—or "unit," as it was called—to assign me to full duty in the work of the club. I was instructed to give my unit a report of my activities; writing, organizing, speaking. I agreed to do this and wrote a report.

A unit, membership in which is obligatory for all Communists, is the party's basic form of organization. Unit meetings are held on certain nights which are kept secret for fear of police raids. Nothing treasonable transpires at these meetings; but, once one is a Communist, one does not have to be guilty of wrongdoing to attract the attention of the police. At these meetings members pay their dues, are given party tasks, are instructed in the party's interpretation of world events.

I went to my first unit meeting—which was held in the Black

Belt of the South Side—and introduced myself to the Negro organizer.

"Welcome, comrade," he said, grinning. "We're glad to have a writer with us."

"I'm not much of a writer," I said.

The meeting started. About twenty Negroes were gathered. The time came for me to make my report and I took out my notes and told them how I had come to join the party, what few stray items I had published, what my duties were in the John Reed Club. I finished and waited for comment. There was silence. I looked about. Most of the comrades sat with bowed heads. Then I was surprised to catch a twitching smile on the lips of a Negro woman. Minutes passed. The Negro woman lifted her head and looked at the organizer. The organizer smothered a smile. Then the woman broke into unrestrained laughter, bending forward and burying her face in her hands. I stared. Had I said something funny?

"What's the matter?" I asked.

The giggling became general. The unit organizer, who had been dallying with his pencil, looked up.

"It's all right, comrade," he said. "We're glad to have a writer in the party."

There was more smothered laughter. Some of the more intelligent ones were striving to keep deadpan faces. What kind of people were these? I had made a serious report and now I heard giggles.

"I did the best I could," I said uneasily. "I realize that writing is not basic or important. But, given time, I think I can make a contribution."

"We know you can, comrade," the black organizer said.

His tone was more patronizing than that of a southern white man. I grew angry. I thought I knew these people, but evidently I did not. I wanted to take issue with their attitude, but caution urged me to talk it over with others first. I left the meeting baffled.

76

During the following days I learned through discreet question-ing that I had seemed a fantastic element to the black Commu-nists. I was shocked to hear that I, who had been only to grammar school, had been classified as an *intellectual*. What was an intel-lectual? I had never heard the word used in the sense in which it was applied to me. I had thought that they might refuse me on the grounds that I was not politically advanced; I had thought they might place me on probation; I had thought they might say I would have to be investigated. But they had simply laughed. And I began to realize why so few sensitive Negroes had had the gall to come as close to them as I had.

I learned, to my dismay, that the black Communists in my unit had commented upon my shined shoes, my clean shirt, and the tie I had worn. Above all, my manner of speech had seemed an alien thing to them.

"He talks like a book," one of the Negro comrades had said.

And that was enough to condemn me forever as bourgeois.

The more I learned of the Negro Communists the more I found that they were not vicious, that they had no intention to hurt. They just did not know anything and did not want to learn anything. They felt that all questions had been answered, and anyone who asked new ones or tried to answer old ones was dangerous. The word "writer" was enough to make a black Chi-cago Communist feel that the man to whom the word applied had gone wrong.

I discovered that it was not wise to be seen reading books that were not endorsed by the Communist party. On one occasion I was asked to show a book that I carried under my arm. The comrade looked at it and shook his head.

"What're you reading this for?" he asked.

"It's interesting," I said.

"Reading bourgeois books can only confuse you, comrade," he said, returning the book.

"You seem convinced that I'm easily confused," I said.

77

"You know," he said, his voice dropping to a low, confidential tone, "many comrades go wrong by reading the books of the bourgeoisie. The party in the Soviet Union had trouble with people like that."

"Didn't Lenin read bourgeois books?" I asked.

"But you're not Lenin," he shot at me.

"Are there some books reserved for some people to read, while others cannot read them?" I asked.

"Comrade, you do not understand," he said.

An invisible wall was building slowly between me and the people with whom I had cast my lot. Well, I would show them that all men who wrote books were not their enemies. I would communicate the meaning of their lives to people whom they could not reach; then, surely, my intentions would merit their confidence. I dismissed the warning about the Soviet Union's trouble with intellectuals. I felt that it simply did not apply to me. The problem I faced seemed a much simpler one. I had to win the confidence of people who had been misled so often that they were afraid of anybody who differed from themselves. Yet deep down I feared their militant ignorance.

In my party work I met a Negro Communist, Ross, who was under indictment for "inciting to riot." I decided to use him in my series of biographical sketches. His trial was pending and he was organizing support in his behalf. Ross was typical of the effective, street agitator. Southern-born, he had migrated north and his life reflected the crude hopes and frustrations of the peasant in the city. Distrustful but aggressive, he was a bundle of the weaknesses and virtues of a man struggling blindly between two societies, of a man living on the margin of a culture. I felt that if I could get his story I would make known some of the difficulties inherent in the adjustment of a folk people to an urban environment; I would make his life more intelligible to others than it was to himself. I would reclaim his disordered days and cast them into a form that people could grasp, see, understand, and accept.

I approached Ross and explained my plan. He was agreeable. He invited me to his home, introduced me to his Jewish wife, his young son, his friends. I talked to Ross for hours, explaining what I was about, cautioning him not to relate anything that he did not want to divulge.

"I'm after the things that made you a Communist," I said.

It was arranged that I was to visit Ross each morning and take notes for two hours. At last, I thought, I would reveal dramas of hope, fear, love, and hate that existed in these humble people. I would make these lives merge with the lives of the mass of mankind. I knew I could. My life had prepared me for this.

Word spread in the Communist party that I was taking notes on the life of Ross and strange things began to happen. A quiet black Communist came to my home one night and called me out to the street to speak to me in private. He made a prediction about my future that frightened me.

"Intellectuals don't fit well into the party, Wright," he said solemnly.

"But I'm not an intellectual," I protested. "I sweep the streets for a living." I had just been assigned by the relief system to sweep the streets for thirteen dollars a week.

"That doesn't make any difference," he said. "We've kept records of the trouble we've had with intellectuals in the past. It's estimated that only 13 per cent of them remain in the party."

"Why do they leave, since you insist upon calling me an intellectual?" I asked.

"Most of them drop out of their own accord," he said.

"Well, I'm not dropping out," I said.

"Some are expelled," he hinted gravely.

"For what?"

"General opposition to the party's policies," he said.

"But I'm not opposing anything in the party."

"But you have to prove yourself."

"What do you mean?"

"You'll have to prove your revolutionary loyalty."

"That's what I'm trying to do through writing."

"That's not the way to do it," he said. "You must act."

"How?"

"The party has a way of testing people."

"Well, talk. What is this?"

"How do you react to police?"

"I don't react to them," I said. "I've never been bothered by them."

"Do you know Evans?" he asked, referring to a local, militant Negro Communist.

"Yes. I've seen him; I've met him."

"Did you notice that he was injured?"

"Yes. His head was bandaged."

"He got that wound from the police in a demonstration," he explained. "That's proof of revolutionary loyalty."

"Do you mean that I must get whacked over the head by cops to prove that I'm sincere?" I asked.

"I'm not suggesting anything," he said. "I'm explaining."

"That's a primitive way to measure sincerity," I gasped.

"It's a practical way," he said.

"Look, suppose a cop whacks me over the head and I suffer a brain concussion. Suppose I'm nuts after that? Can I write then? What will I have proven?"

He did not answer. He shook his head.

"The Soviet Union has had to shoot a lot of intellectuals," he said.

"Good God!" I exclaimed. "Do you know what you're saying? You're not in Russia. You're standing on a sidewalk in Chicago. You talk like a man lost in a fantasy."

He said nothing. I did not know that the notes I was taking of Ross's life were being discussed by the local Communist leaders, that my motives were already being questioned; and no doubt my rash words did not help any.

"You've heard of Trotsky, haven't you?" he asked.

"Yes."

"Do you know what happened to him?"

"He was banished from the Soviet Union," I said.

"Do you know why?"

"Well," I stammered, trying not to reveal my ignorance of politics, for I had not followed the details of Trotsky's fight against the Communist party of the Soviet Union, "it seems that after a decision had been made, he broke that decision by organizing against the party."

"It was for counterrevolutionary activity," he snapped impatiently; I learned afterwards that my answer had not been satisfactory, had not been couched in the acceptable phrases of bitter, anti-Trotsky denunciation.

"I understand," I said. "But I've never read Trotsky. What's his stand on minorities?"

"Why ask me?" he asked. "I don't read Trotsky."

"Look," I asked, "if you found me reading Trotsky, what would that mean to you?"

"You have no need to read Trotsky," he said.

"Don't you think I can read Trotsky and not be influenced to follow him?" I asked.

"Comrade, you don't understand," he said in an annoyed tone.

That ended the conversation. But that was not the last time I was to hear the phrase: "Comrade, you don't understand." I had not been aware of holding wrong ideas. I had not read any of Trotsky's works; indeed, the very opposite had been true. It had been Stalin's *The National and Colonial Question* that had captured my interest.

Stalin's book showed how diverse minorities could be welded

into unity, and I regarded it as a most politically sensitive volume that revealed a new way of looking upon lost and beaten peoples. Of all the developments in the Soviet Union, the method by which scores of backward peoples had been led to unity on a national scale was what had enthralled me. I had read with awe how the Communists had sent phonetic experts into the vast regions of Russia to listen to the stammering dialects of peoples oppressed for centuries by the czars. I had made the first total emotional commitment of my life when I read how the phonetic experts had given these tongueless people a language, newspapers, institutions. I had read how these forgotten folk had been encouraged to keep their old cultures, to see in their ancient customs meanings and satisfactions as deep as those contained in supposedly superior ways of living. And I had exclaimed to myself how different this was from the way in which Negroes were sneered at in America.

Then what was the meaning of the warning I had received from the black Communist? Why was it that I was a suspected man because I wanted to reveal the vast physical and spiritual ravages of Negro life, the profundity latent in these rejected people, the dramas as old as man and the sun and the mountains and the seas that were transpiring in the poverty of black America? What was the danger in showing the kinship between the sufferings of the Negro and the sufferings of other people?

I sat one morning in Ross's home with his wife and child. I was scribbling furiously upon my yellow sheets of paper. The doorbell rang and Ross's wife admitted a black Communist, one Ed Green. He was tall, taciturn, soldierly, square-shouldered. I was introduced to him and he nodded stiffly.

"What's happening here?" he asked bluntly.

Ross explained my project to him, and as Ross talked I could see Ed Green's face darken. He had not sat down and when Ross's wife offered him a chair, he did not hear her.

"What're you going to do with these notes?" he asked me.

"I hope to weave them into stories," I said.

"What're you asking the party members?"

"About their lives in general."

"Who suggested this to you?" he asked.

"Nobody. I thought of it myself."

"Were you ever a member of any other political group?"

"I worked with the Republicans once," I said.

"I mean, revolutionary organizations?" he asked.

"No. Why do you ask?"

"What kind of work do you do?"

"I sweep the streets for a living."

"How far did you go in school?"

"Through the grammar grades."

"You talk like a man who went further than that," he said.

"Why would I lie to you about my education?" I asked.

"I don't know," he said, looking directly at me.

"I've read books. I taught myself."

"You know about Ross's indictment?" he asked.

"Yes."

"I don't know," he said, looking off.

"What do you mean?" I asked. "What's wrong?"

"To whom have you shown this material?"

"I've shown it to no one yet."

What was the meaning of his questions? Naïvely I thought that he himself would make a good model for a biographical sketch.

"I'd like to interview you next," I said.

"I'm not interested," he snapped.

His manner was so rough that I did not urge him. He called Ross into a rear room. I sat feeling that I was guilty of something. In a few minutes Ed Green returned, stared at me wordlessly, then marched out.

"Who does he think he is?" I asked Ross.

"He's a member of the Central Committee," Ross said.

"But why does he act like that?"

"Oh, he's always like that," Ross said uneasily.

There was a long silence.

"He's wondering what you're doing with this material," Ross said finally.

I looked at him. He, too, had been captured by suspicion. He was trying to hide the fear in his face.

"You don't have to tell me anything you don't want to," I said.

That seemed to soothe him for a moment. But the seed of doubt had already been planted. I felt dizzy. Was I mad? Or were these people mad?

"You see, Dick," Ross's wife said, "Ross is under an indictment. Ed Green is the representative of the International Labor Defense for the South Side. It's his duty to keep track of the people he's trying to defend. He wanted to know if Ross has given you anything that could be used against him in court."

I was speechless.

"What does he think I am?" I demanded.

There was no answer.

"You lost people!" I cried and banged my fist on the table.

Ross was shaken and ashamed.

"Aw, Ed Green's just supercautious," he mumbled.

"Ross," I asked, "do you trust me?"

"Oh, yes," he said uneasily.

We two black men sat in the same room looking at each other in fear. Both of us were hungry. Both of us depended upon public charity to eat and for a place to sleep. Yet we had more doubt in our hearts of each other than of the men who had cast the mold of our lives.

Self-consciously we went on with the work, but something was gone out of it. Did they think I was gathering material for the police? How could I make them understand what I was trying to do? I found that when I talked to them in abstract terms, my ideas were not understood. The irony of it was that I, who had all but to steal books to read, had been branded as an intellectual by the one group that claimed it was dedicated to educating the oppressed and informing them with a vision of life. I was doubted by those who shared more of my life than any others could possibly share of it.

I could not doubt the sincerity of Ed Green. His was a long and militant record in the Communist party. Then why was he suspicious of me? And, if he doubted me, whom could he ever trust? If I was an intellectual, then what was a Negro doctor, lawyer, teacher? The thing just did not make sense. Yet there it was . . .

Ed Green was afterwards killed in action while fighting for the Spanish Loyalists. He knew how to die better than he knew how to live. He was organically capable of only the most elementary reactions. His fear-haunted life made him suspicious of everything that did not look as he looked, that did not act as he acted, that did not talk as he talked, that did not feel as he felt. His existence both gladdened and frightened me. I was glad that he was militant, but I was frightened when I pondered upon what he could do with his militancy. The only people he could move to believe in him were those who shared his own world of fear, and all the world that lay beyond his terribly restricted vision was enemy ground.

I wanted to make the lives of these men known through the images already accepted as the common coin of communication. I wanted to make them know that they had allies, that more people than they knew, and in ways they did not understand, were their friends, and that I was their friend. I wanted to voice the words in them that they could not say, to be a witness for their living. And they were wondering if I were in league with the police!

85

I had embraced their aims with the freest impulse I had ever known. I, the chary cynic, the man who had felt that no idea on earth was worthy of self-sacrifice, had publicly identified myself with them, and now their suspicion of me hit me with a terrific impact, froze me within. I groped in the noon sun. What was I after? they wanted to know. And when I tried to explain, I always, it seemed, said the wrong things. There were no concrete charges that they could bring against me. They were simply afraid of that which was not familiar. They were more fearful of my ideas than they would have been had I held a gun on them; they could have taken the gun away from me and shot me with it, but they did not know what to do with ideas.

I talked with white Communists about my experiences with black Communists, and I could not make them understand what I was talking about. White Communists had idealized all Negroes to the extent that they did not see the same Negroes I saw. And the more I tried to explain my ideas the more they, too, began to suspect that I was somehow dreadfully wrong. Words lost their usual meanings. Simple motives took on sinister colors. Attitudes underwent quick and startling transformations. Ideas turned into their opposites while you were talking to a person you thought you knew. I began to feel an emotional isolation that I had not known in the depths of the hate-ridden South.

I continued to take notes on Ross's life, but each successive morning found him more reticent. I pitied him and did not argue with him, for I knew that persuasion would not nullify his fears. Instead I sat and listened to him and his friends tell tales of southern Negro experience, noting them down in my mind, not daring to ask questions for fear they would become alarmed. In spite of their fears, I became quite drenched in the details of their lives. I gave up the idea of the biographical sketches and settled finally upon writing a series of short stories, using the material I had got from Ross and his friends, building upon it, inventing. I wove a tale of a group of black boys trespassing upon the property of a white man and the lynching that followed. The story was published in an anthology under the title of *Big Boy Leaves Home*, but its appearance came too late to influence the Communists who were questioning the use to which I was putting their lives.

My fitful work assignments from the relief officials ceased and I looked for work that did not exist. I borrowed money to ride to and fro on the club's business. I found a cramped attic for my mother and aunt and brother behind some railroad tracks. At last the relief authorities placed me in the South Side Boys' Club and my wages were just enough to provide a deficient diet.

Then political problems rose to plague me. Ross, whose life I had tried to write, was charged by the Communist party with "anti-leadership tendencies," "class collaborationist attitudes," and "ideological factionalism," phrases so fanciful that I gaped when I heard them. And it was rumored that I, too, would face similar charges. It was known that I had visited Ross, had taken notes on his life, and it was believed that I had been politically influenced by him, though in what way was not stated. As before, the more I tried to explain the guiltier I seemed in the eyes of my comrades. I had taken part in the formation of none of the policies of the Communist party, had expressed no opinion regarding its leadership or work. But the rumors of my disaffection persisted.

One night a group of black comrades came to my house and warned me against believing in Ross's ideas. When I assured them that I did not share Ross's views, they ordered me to stay away from him.

"But why?" I demanded.

"He's an unhealthy element," they said. "Can't you accept a decision?"

"Is this a decision of the Communist party?"

"Yes," they said.

"If I were guilty of something, I'd feel bound to keep your decision," I said. "But I've done nothing."

"Comrade, you don't understand," they said. "Members of the party do not violate the party's decisions."

"But your decision does not apply to me," I said. "I'll be damned if I'll act as if it does."

"Your attitude does not merit our trust," they said.

I was angry.

"Look," I exploded, rising and sweeping my arms at the bleak attic in which I lived, "what is it here that frightens you? You know where I work! You know what I earn! You know my friends! Now, what in God's name is wrong?"

They left with mirthless smiles which implied that I would soon know what was wrong.

But there was relief from these shadowy political bouts. I found my work in the South Side Boys' Club deeply engrossing. Each day black boys between the ages of eight and twenty-five came to swim, draw, and read. They were a wild and homeless lot, culturally lost, spiritually disinherited, candidates for the clinics, morgues, prisons, reformatories, and the electric chair of the state's death house. For hours I listened to their talk of planes, women, guns, politics, and crime. Their figures of speech were as forceful and colorful as any ever used by English-speaking people. I kept pencil and paper in my pocket to jot down their word-rhythms and reactions. These boys did not fear people to the extent that every man looked like a spy. The Communists who doubted my motives did not know these boys, their twisted dreams, their all-too-clear destinies; and I doubted if I would ever be able to convey to them the tragedy I saw here.

Wrestling with words gave me my moments of deepest meaning. The short story, *Big Boy Leaves Home*, had posed a question:

What quality of will must a Negro possess to live and die with dignity in a country that denied his humanity? There took shape in my mind—as though an answer was trying to grope its way out of the depths of me—the tale of a flood, *Down by the Riverside*. I waded into it, feeling my way, trying to find the answer to my question. But it dissatisfied me when I had finished it; so, casting it aside, I tried to say the same thing in yet another way in *Long Black Song*. But that did not catch the quality of the experience I was looking for.

Party duties broke into my efforts at expression. The club decided upon a conference of all the left-wing writers in the Middle West. I supported the idea and argued that the conference should deal with craft problems. My arguments were rejected. The conference, the club decided, would deal with political questions. I asked for a definition of what was expected from the writers, books or political activity. Both, was the answer. Write a few hours a day and march on the picket line the other hours. I pointed out that the main concern of a revolutionary artist was to produce revolutionary art, and that the future of the club was in doubt if a clear policy could not be found.

The conference convened with a leading Communist attending as adviser. The question debated was: What did the Communist party expect from the club? The answer of the Communist leader ran from organizing to writing novels. I argued that either a man organized or he wrote novels. The party leader said that both must be done. The attitude of the party leader prevailed and *Left Front*, for which I had worked so long, was voted out of existence.

The party leader demanded that writers be assigned the task of producing pamphlets for the use of trade unions. I contended that it would be a mistake for the Communist party to persuade writers to abandon imaginative work to write pamphlets. I explained the advantages that could be derived from the long-term artistic products of the club's writers, and pointed out that these more durable products would outweigh all the pamphleteering. This, too, was rejected by vote. I then appealed for an organizational structure that would include provisions for artistic work of all types, hoping in this way to eliminate constant quarrels over tactics and strategy. But all my proposals were voted down.

I knew now that the club was nearing its end, and I rose and stated my gloomy conclusions, recommending that the club dissolve. My "defeatism," as it was called, brought upon my head the sharpest disapproval of the party leader. The conference ended with the passing of a multitude of resolutions dealing with China, India, Germany, Japan, and conditions afflicting various parts of the earth. But not one idea regarding writing had emerged.

The ideas I had expounded at the conference were linked with the suspicions I had roused among the Negro Communists on the South Side, and the Communist party was now certain that it had a dangerous enemy in its midst. It was whispered that I was trying to lead a secret group in opposition to the party. I had learned that denial of accusations was useless. It was now painful to meet a Communist, for I did not know what his attitude would be.

Following the conference, a national John Reed Club congress was called. It convened in the summer of 1934 with left-wing writers attending from all states. But, as the sessions got under way, there was a sense of looseness, bewilderment, and dissatisfaction among the writers, most of whom were young, eager, and on the verge of doing their best work. No one knew what was expected of him, and out of the congress came no unifying idea. Through conversations I learned that the members of the New York John Reed Club were in despair at the way in which the congress was drifting, but they took care to conceal their disapproval. This puzzled me, for I felt that the problem should be brought into the open for discussion. But I was glad to hear the New York Communists express horror at the brutal way in which the Chicago Communists made demands upon the Chicago John Reed Club membership. One astonished New York comrade declared:

"A Chicago Communist is a walking terror!"

As the congress drew to a close, I attended a caucus to plan the future of the clubs. Ten of us met in a Loop hotel room and, to my amazement, the leaders of the club's national board confirmed my criticisms of the manner in which the clubs had been conducted. I was excited. Now, I thought, the clubs will be given a new lease on life. Writers would now be free to make their political contributions in the form of their creative work.

Then I was stunned when I heard a nationally known Communist announce a decision to dissolve the clubs. Why? I asked. Because the clubs do not serve the new People's Front policy, I was told. That can be remedied; the clubs can be made healthy and broad, I said. No; a bigger and better organization must be launched, one in which the leading writers of the nation could be included, they said. I was informed that the People's Front policy was now the correct vision of life and that the clubs could no longer exist. I asked what was to become of the young writers whom the Communist party had implored to join the clubs and who were ineligible for the new group, and there was no answer. This thing is cold! I exclaimed to myself. To effect a swift change in policy, the Communist party was dumping one organization, scattering its members, then organizing a new scheme with entirely new people!

I had sacrificed energy to recruit writers who subscribed to a revolutionary point of view, and now my feelings fought against the waste and meaninglessness to which my efforts were being reduced. This was the first time I had sat with a Communist policymaking body; I had had the illusion that each man would

91

have his say and, out of the facts presented, a decision would be made. I was naïve. I had merely been called in to give my approval to a decision previously made. It angered me.

I found myself arguing alone against the majority opinion and then I made still another amazing discovery. I saw that even those who agreed with me would not support me. At that meeting I learned that when a man was informed of the wish of the party he submitted, even though he knew with all the strength of his brain that the wish was not a wise one, was one that would ultimately harm the party's interests. I had heard Communists discuss discipline in the abstract, but when I saw it in its concrete form it tore my feelings.

It was not courage that made me oppose the party. I simply did not know any better. It was inconceivable to me, though bred in the lap of southern hate, that a man could not have his say. I had spent a third of my life traveling from the place of my birth to the North just to talk freely, to escape the pressure of fear. And now I was facing fear again, though I had no notion that I was slowly adding fagots to a flame that would soon blaze over my head with all the violence of the assault I had sustained when I had naïvely thought I could learn the optical trade in Mississippi.

(The artist and the politician stand at opposite poles. The artist enhances life by his prolonged concentration upon it, while the politician emphasizes the impersonal aspect of life by his attempts to fit men into groups. The artist's enhancement of life may emphasize, at certain times, those aspects that a politician can use. But the politician, at other times, eager to do good for man, may sneer at the artist because the art product cannot be used by him. Hence, the two groups of men, driving in the same direction, committed to the same vision, often find themselves locked in a struggle more desperate than either of them wanted, while their mutual enemies gape at the spectacle in amazement.

(Why did not we writers leave the realm of politics and organize ourselves? We simply did not know how. We were hostile toward our environment and we did not know how other American writers had met such problems. Totally at odds with our culture, we wanted nothing less than to make anew; and, for our examples, we looked toward Russia, Germany, and France. Out of step with our times, it was but natural for us to respond to the Communist party, which said: "Your rebellion is right. Come with us and we will support your vision with militant action."

(Indeed, we felt that we were lucky. Why cower in towers of ivory and squeeze out private words when we had only to speak and millions listened? Our writing was translated into French, German, Russian, Chinese, Spanish, Japanese . . . Who had ever, in all human history, offered to young writers an audience so vast? True, our royalties were small or less than small, but that did not matter.

(We wrote what we felt. Confronted with a picture of a revolutionary and changing world, there spilled out of our hearts our reaction to that world, our hope, our anger at oppression, our dreams of a new life; it spilled without coercion, without the pleading of anyone.)

Before the congress adjourned, it was decided that another congress of American writers would be called in New York the following summer, 1935. I was lukewarm to the proposal and tried to make up my mind to stand alone, write alone. I was already afraid that the stories I had written would not fit into the new, official mood. Must I discard my plot-ideas and seek new ones? No. I could not. My writing was my way of seeing, my way of living, my way of feeling; and who could change his sight, his notion of direction, his senses?

My relationship with Communists reached a static phase. I shunned them and they shunned me. Buddy Nealson, a member of the Communist International, had arrived in Chicago to assume charge of Negro work. This man, it was rumored, was the party's theoretician on the Negro Question, and word reached me that he had launched a campaign to rid the Communist party of all its "Negro Trotskyite elements." Of all the Negro Communists I knew, I tried to determine who could be called Trotskyite, and I could think of none. None of the black Communists I knew possessed the intellectual capacity to formulate a Trotskyite position in politics. Most of them were illiterate migrants from southern plantations and they had never been vitally interested in politics until they had entered the Communist party. Nevertheless, the drive against Negro Trotskyism went on, though I was too remote from it to know what was happening.

The spring of 1935 came and the plans for the writers' congress went on apace. For some obscure reason—it might have been to "save" me—I was urged by the local Communists to attend and I was named as a delegate. I got time off from my job at the South Side Boys' Club and, along with several other delegates, hitchhiked to New York.

Long used to the flat western prairie, I was startled by my first view of New York. We came in along the Hudson River and I stared at the sweep of clean-kept homes and grounds. But where was the smoke pall? The soot? Grain elevators? Factories? Stackpipes? The flashes of steam on the horizon? The people on the sidewalks seemed better dressed than the people of Chicago. Their eyes were bold and impersonal. They walked with a quicker stride and seemed intent upon reaching some destination in a great hurry.

We arrived in the early evening and registered for the congress sessions. The opening mass meeting was being held at Carnegie Hall. I asked about housing accommodations and the New York John Reed Club members, all white members of the Communist party, looked embarrassed. I waited while one white Communist called another white Communist to one side and discussed what could be done to get me, a black Chicago Communist, housed. During the trip I had not thought of myself as a Negro; I had been mulling over the problems of the young left-wing writers I knew. Now, as I stood watching one white comrade talk frantically to another about the color of my skin, I felt disgusted. The white comrade returned.

"Just a moment, comrade," he said to me. "I'll get a place for you."

"But haven't you places already?" I asked. "Matters of this sort are ironed out in advance."

"Yes," he admitted in an intimate tone. "We have some addresses here, but we don't know the people. You understand?"

"Yes, I understand," I said, gritting my teeth.

"But just wait a second," he said, touching my arm to reassure me. "I'll find something."

"Listen, don't bother," I said, trying to keep anger out of my voice.

"Oh, no," he said, shaking his head determinedly. "This is a problem and I'll solve it."

"It oughtn't to be a problem," I could not help saying.

"Oh, I didn't mean that," he caught himself quickly.

Goddamn, I cursed under my breath. Several people standing near-by observed the white Communist trying to find a black Communist a place to sleep. I burned with shame. A few minutes later the white Communist returned, frantic-eyed, sweating.

"Did you find anything?" I asked.

"No, not yet," he said, panting. "Just a moment. I'm going to call somebody I know. Say, give me a nickel for the phone."

"Forget it," I said. My legs felt like water. "I'll find a place. But I'd like to put my suitcase somewhere until after the meeting tonight."

"Do you really think you can find a place?" he asked, trying to keep a note of desperate hope out of his voice.

"Of course, I can," I said.

He was still uncertain. He wanted to help me, but he did not know how. He locked my bag in a closet and I stepped to the sidewalk wondering where Harlem was, wondering where I would sleep that night. Before I had left Chicago I had thought of a thousand arguments to present for the retention of the John Reed Clubs, but now the retention of those clubs did not seem important. I stood on the sidewalks of New York with a black skin, practically no money, and I was not absorbed with the burning questions of the left-wing literary movement in the United States, but with the problem of how to get a bath. I presented my credentials at Carnegie Hall. The building was jammed with people. As I listened to the militant speeches, I found myself wondering why in hell I had come.

I went to the sidewalk and stood studying the faces of the people. The white Communist who had been scouting for a room in which I could sleep ran up to me.

"Did you find a place yet?"

"No," I answered.

"Well, here's a name and address," he said proudly. "Go there and they'll put you up for tonight."

"Thanks," I said, glad to have a place to flop.

When the meeting ended, I retrieved my bag from the club, and found the address in a dark alley of Greenwich Village. I knocked at the door. A white man opened it, took one quick look at my face, then pushed the door almost shut again, as though in desperate defense of himself and his home.

"What do you want?" the words spilled out of him.

I asked for the person whose name was written on the slip of paper I had.

"They aren't here," he said.

"When will they return?" I asked.

"I don't know," he spluttered, inching the door to.

96

I walked away. How could I sleep in a home where the sight of my face struck fear into people? I returned to the club and saw a few of the white comrades standing about the sidewalk. I crossed to the opposite side of the street to avoid them. I approached a newsstand merchant. It was nearing three o'clock.

"Where is Harlem?" I asked.

He stared at me. I lost my temper.

"For God's sake!" I exploded. "I'm a stranger here. I'm asking you where Harlem is!"

He blinked and pointed vaguely.

"That way," he said.

His directions did not help me. I walked on. I met a Chicago club member.

"Didn't you find a place yet?" he asked.

"No," I said. "I'd like to try one of the hotels, but, God, I'm in no mood to argue with a hotel clerk about my color."

"Oh, goddamn, wait a minute," he said.

I waited as he scooted off. He returned in a few moments with a big heavy white woman. He introduced us.

"You can sleep in my place, tonight," she said.

I walked with her to her apartment and she introduced me to her husband. I thanked them for their hospitality and went to sleep on a cot in the kitchen. I got up at six, dressed, tapped on their door and bade them good-bye. I went to the sidewalk, sat on a bench, took out pencil and paper and tried to jot down notes for the argument I wanted to make in defense of the John Reed Clubs. But again the problem of the clubs did not seem important. What did seem important was: Could a Negro ever live halfway like a human being in this goddamn country?

That day I sat through the congress sessions, but what I heard did not touch me. That night I found my way to Harlem and walked pavements filled with black life. I was amazed, when I asked passers-by, to learn that there were practically no hotels for

Negroes in Harlem. I kept walking. Finally I saw a tall, clean hotel; black people were passing the doors and no white people were in sight. Confidently I entered and was surprised to see a white clerk behind the desk. I hesitated.

"I'd like a room," I said.

"Not here," he said.

"But isn't this Harlem?" I asked.

"Yes, but this hotel is for white only," he said.

"Where is a hotel for colored?"

"You might try the Y," he said.

"In what direction is it?"

"Keep walking that way," he said, pointing.

Half an hour later I found the Negro Young Men's Christian Association, that bulwark of Jim Crowism for young black men, got a room, took a bath, and slept for twelve hours. When I awakened, I did not want to go to the congress. I lay in bed thinking: I've got to go it alone . . . I've got to learn how again . . .

I dressed and attended the meeting that was to make the final decision to dissolve the clubs. It started briskly. A New York Communist writer summed up the history of the clubs and made a motion for their dissolution. Debate started and I rose and explained what the clubs had meant to young writers and begged for their continuance. I sat down amid silence. Debate was closed. The vote was called. The room filled with uplifted hands to dissolve. Then there came a call for those who disagreed and my hand went up alone. I knew that my stand would be interpreted as one of opposition to the Communist party, but I thought: The hell with it . . .

New York held no further interest and the next morning I left for home.

With the clubs now dissolved, I was free of all party relations. I avoided unit meetings for fear of being subjected to discipline.

Occasionally a Negro Communist—defying the code that enjoined him to shun suspect elements—came to my home and informed me of the current charges that Communists were bringing against one another. To my astonishment I heard that Buddy Nealson had branded me a "smuggler of reaction."

"Why does he call me that?" I asked.

"He says that you are a petty bourgeois degenerate," I was told.

"What does that mean?"

"He says that you are corrupting the party with your ideas," I was told.

"How?"

There was no answer. I decided that my relationship with the party was about over; I would have to leave it. The attacks were growing worse, and my refusal to react incited Nealson into coining more absurd phrases. I was termed a "bastard intellectual," an "incipient Trotskyite"; it was claimed that I possessed an "anti-leadership attitude" and that I was manifesting "seraphim tendencies," the latter phrase meaning that one has withdrawn from the struggle of life and considers oneself an infallible angel.

I could not dismiss these charges lightly, for a frantic, hysterical hunt was going on in the ranks of the party for Trotskyites. In the Soviet Union men were being shot for Trotskyism. I used to lie awake nights wondering what would happen to me if I lived in the Soviet Union.

Working all day and writing half the night brought me down with a severe chest ailment. I was in constant pain, scarcely able to breathe. I lay reviewing the life I had lived in the party and I found it distasteful. I realized that I had not been objective in my quixotic fight to save the clubs. I had been fighting as much for myself as for them. But was that wrong? Again I resolved to leave the party, for the emotional cost of membership was too high.

While I was ill, a knock came at my door one morning. My mother admitted Ed Green, the man who had demanded to know what use I planned to make of the material I was collecting from the comrades. I stared at him as I lay abed and I knew that he considered me a clever and sworn enemy of the party. Bitterness welled up in me.

"What do you want?" I asked bluntly. "You see I'm ill."

"I have a message from the party for you," he said.

I had not said good day, and he had not offered to say it. He had not smiled, and neither had I. He looked curiously at my bleak room.

"This is the home of a bastard intellectual," I cut at him.

He stared without blinking. I could not endure his standing there so stone-like. Common decency made me say:

"Sit down."

His shoulders stiffened.

"I'm in a hurry." He spoke like an army officer.

"What do you want to tell me?"

"Do you know Buddy Nealson?" he asked.

"No," I said. "But I've heard of him."

I was suspicious. Was this a political trap? They had hurled baseless accusations at me and I felt that there could be no ground of trust between us. Was he trying to discover if I knew someone whom, politically, I should not know? But, after all, Buddy Nealson was a member of the Communist International. But what if Buddy Nealson had suddenly been accused of something and Ed Green was here trying to find out if I knew him?

"What about Buddy Nealson?" I asked, committing myself to nothing until I knew the kind of reality I was grappling with.

"He wants to see you," Ed Green said.

I breathed easier. I could not meet Communists now without feeling a degree of fear.

"What about?" I asked, still suspicious.

"He wants to talk with you about your party work," he said.

"I'm ill and can't see him until I'm well," I said.

Ed Green stood for a fraction of a second, then turned on his heel and marched out of the room.

Ought I see Buddy Nealson? He was the man who had formulated the Communist position for the American Negro; he had made speeches in the Kremlin; he had spoken before Stalin himself. Then perhaps he could explain many of the aspects of Communism that had baffled me. Anyway, I resolved to confront him and ask him some direct, simple questions and hear what he had to say.

When my chest healed, I sought an appointment with Buddy Nealson. He was a short, black man with an ever-ready smile, thick lips, a furtive manner, and a greasy, sweaty look. His bearing was nervous, self-conscious; he seemed always to be hiding some deep irritation. He spoke in short, jerky sentences, hopping nimbly from thought to thought, as though his mind worked in a free, associational manner. He suffered from asthma and would snort at unexpected intervals. Now and then he would punctuate his flow of words by taking a nip from a bottle of whisky. He had traveled half around the world and his talk was pitted with vague allusions to European cities. I met him in his apartment, listened to him intently, observed him minutely, for I knew that I was facing one of the leaders of World Communism.

"Hello, Wright," he snorted. "I've heard about you."

As we shook hands he burst into a loud, seemingly causeless laugh; and as he guffawed I could not tell whether his mirth was directed at me or was meant to hide his uneasiness.

"I hope what you've heard about me is good," I parried.

"Sit down," he laughed again, waving me to a chair. "Yes, they tell me you write . . ."

"I try to," I said.

"You can write," he snorted. "I read that article you wrote for the *New Masses* about Joe Louis. Good stuff . . . First political treatment of sports we've yet had. Ha-ha . . ."

"I'm trying to reveal the meaning of Negro experience," I said.

"We need a man like you," he said flatteringly.

I waited. I had thought that I would encounter a man of ideas, but he was not that. Then perhaps he was a man of action? But that was not indicated either. As we talked, I tried to grasp the frame of reference of his words, so that I would know how to talk to him.

"They tell me that you are a friend of Ross," he shot at me.

I paused before answering. He had not asked me directly, but had hinted in a neutral, teasing way. Mentally I prodded myself into remembering that I was speaking to a member of the Communist International. Ross, I had been told, was slated for expulsion on the grounds that he was "anti-leadership"; and if a member of the Communist International was asking me if I were a friend of a man about to be expelled, he was indirectly asking me if I were loyal or not.

"Ross is not particularly a friend of mine," I said frankly. "But I know him well; in fact, quite well."

"If he isn't your friend, how do you happen to know him so well?" he asked, laughing to soften the hard threat of his question.

"I was writing an account of his life and I know him as well, perhaps, as anybody," I told him.

"I heard about that," he said. "Wright . . . Ha-ha . . . Say, let me call you Dick, hunh?"

"Go ahead," I said.

"Dick," he said, "Ross is a nationalist." He paused to let the weight of his accusation sink in. He meant that Ross's militancy was extreme. "We Communists don't dramatize Negro nationalism," he said in a voice that laughed, accused, and drawled.

"What do you mean?" I asked.

"We're not advertising Ross." He spoke directly now.

"We're talking about two different things," I said. "You seem worried about my making Ross popular because he is your political opponent. But I'm not concerned about Ross's politics at all. The man struck me as one who typified certain traits of the Negro migrant. I've already sold a story based upon an incident in his life."

Nealson became excited.

"What was the incident?" he asked.

"Some trouble he got into when he was thirteen years old," I said.

His face looked blank for a second, then he laughed.

"Oh, I thought it was political," he said, shrugging.

"But I'm telling you that you are wrong about that," I explained. "I'm not trying to fight you with my writing. I've no political ambitions. I'm not trying to hurt or help any particular comrade. You must believe that. I'm trying to depict Negro life."

"Have you finished writing about Ross?" he asked.

"No," I said. "I dropped the idea. Our party members were suspicious of me and were afraid to talk."

He laughed.

"You've got to know us better, Dick," he grinned. "I hold a high position in the party. I'll straighten out this misunderstanding."

"I'm not looking for a patron," I said.

"I don't mean that," he said, grinning, snorting. "Here, Dick, hava drink."

"No, thank you."

"Don't you drink?"

"Sometimes."

There are men with whom one can drink and there are men with whom one cannot drink. Nealson was one of the men with whom I could not drink. He drank and put the bottle back; he shot me a quick, self-conscious glance. I was tense, but rigidly controlled.

"Dick," he began, "we're short of forces. We're facing a grave crisis."

"The party's always facing a crisis," I said.

His smile left and he stared at me.

"You're not cynical, are you, Dick?" he asked.

"No," I said. "But it's the truth. Each week, each month there's a crisis."

"You're a funny guy," he said, laughing, snorting again. "But we've got a job to do. We're altering our work. Fascism's the danger, the danger now to all people."

"I understand," I said.

"You were in New York not long ago," he said unexpectedly.

"Yes."

"Did you talk with any of the party leaders?"

"No."

"You said nothing to anyone about your work here?"

I stared at him. Was he trying to find out whether I had taken up any of his accusations with the national leadership of the party? Was he trying to determine whether I had influential enough political connections to make trouble for him?

"I told you that I have no political ambitions," I said.

"Yes," he said. "They say that you didn't want the clubs dissolved."

"No, I didn't," I said truthfully. "I felt that the ground was being cut from under the feet of the party's best writers."

"We've got to defeat the Fascists," he said, snorting from asthma, switching his line of thought. "We've discussed you and know your abilities. We want you to work with us. We've got to crash out of our narrow way of working, and get our message to the church people, students, club people, professionals, middle class . . ."

"I've been called names," I said softly. "Is that crashing out of the narrow way?"

"Forget that," he said, laughing.

He had not denied the name-calling. That meant that, if I did not obey him, the name-calling would begin again.

"I don't know if I fit into things," I said openly.

"We want to trust you with an important assignment," he said.

"What do you want me to do?"

"We want you to organize a committee against the high cost of living . . ."

"The high cost of living?" I exclaimed. "What do I know about such things?"

"It's easy. You can learn," he said.

I was in the midst of writing a novel and he was calling me from it to tabulate the price of groceries. He doesn't think much of what I'm trying to do, I thought.

"Comrade Nealson," I said, "a writer who hasn't written anything worth-while is a most doubtful person. Now, I'm in that category. Yet I think I can write. I don't want to ask for special favors, but I'm in the midst of a book which I hope to complete in six months or so. Let me convince myself that I'm wrong about my hankering to write and then I'll be with you all the way."

"The party can't wait," he said. "You'll find time to write."

"I work every day for a living," I said, remembering that he was being paid by the party to talk to me.

"Look, we want to make you a mass leader," he said.

"But suppose I'm not that kind of material?"

He laughed. Not one word that I had said had been seriously considered by him. Our talk was a game; he was trying to outwit me. The feelings of others meant nothing to him.

"Dick," he said, turning in his chair and waving his hand as though to brush away an insect that was annoying him, "you've got to get to the masses of people . . ."

"You've seen some of my work," I said. "Isn't it just barely good enough to warrant my being given a chance?"

"The party can't deal with your feelings," he said.

"Maybe I don't belong in the party." I stated it in full.

"Oh, no! Don't say that," he said, snorting. He looked at me. "You're blunt."

"I put things the way I feel them," I said. "I want to start in right with you. I've had too damn much crazy trouble in the party."

He laughed and lit a cigarette.

"Dick," he said, shaking his head, "the trouble with you is that you've been around with those white artists on the North Side too much . . . You even talk like 'em. You've got to know your own people . . ."

"I think I know them," I said, realizing that I could never really talk with him. "I've been inside of three-fourths of the Negroes' homes on the South Side . . .

"But you've got to work with 'em," he said.

"I was working with Ross until I was suspected of being a spy," I said.

There was silence. The doorbell rang and he admitted his wife, a dark, attractive, European white woman who carried a book under her arm. She came forward with a wide smile. Nealson introduced us.

"What are you reading?" I asked.

"A Dracula mystery story," she said, eagerly exhibiting her book. "You know, Dick, you and I ought to build Negro culture on the South Side."

"I'm asking Nealson for that chance right now," I said, wondering what connection there could be between a Dracula mystery and Negro culture.

"I want him to organize against high prices," Nealson told his wife. "But he's writing a book . . ."

"That oughtn't interfere with his book," she said, sliding easily into a verbal solution of my problem.

"I work in the day," I said.

"Oh, you'll find time," she said lightly.

She left the room and there was silence. The next word was due to come from the member of the Communist International.

"Dick," he spoke seriously now, "the party has decided that you are to accept this task."

I was silent. I knew the meaning of what he had said. A decision was the highest injunction that a Communist could receive from his party, and to break a decision was to break the effectiveness of the party's ability to act. In principle I heartily agreed with this, for I knew that it was impossible for working people to forge instruments of political power until they had achieved unity of action. Oppressed for centuries, divided, hopeless, corrupted, misled, they were cynical—as I had once been—and the Communist method of unity had been found historically to be the only means of achieving discipline. In short, Nealson had asked me directly if I were a Communist or not. I wanted to be a Communist, but my kind of Communist. I wanted to shape people's feelings, awaken their hearts. But I could not tell Nealson that; he would only have snorted.

"I'll organize the committee and turn it over to someone else," I suggested.

"You don't want to do this, do you?" he asked.

"No," I said firmly.

"You worked willingly enough to organize white writers," he cut at me.

"I was organizing people I understood," I said.

"What would you like to do on the South Side, then?"

"I'd like to organize Negro artists," I said.

"But the party doesn't need that now," he said.

I rose, knowing that he had no intention of letting me go after I had organized the committee. I wanted to tell him that I was through, but I was not ready to bring matters to a head. I went out, angry with myself, angry with him, angry with the party. Well, I had not broken the decision, but neither had I accepted it wholly. I had dodged, trying to save time for writing, time to think.

Again I urged myself to quit, but I could not do it. I knew that Nealson was not a leader. His mind was too rigid, too limited. I had not discerned in him any understanding of life or politics. His

107

approach had been to offer me a drink, and when that had failed he had threatened; he had tried flattery, and when that had failed he had hinted at expulsion. If I had been wrong, he certainly had not convinced me. In the end I resolved to work a month, then confront him with my original compromise.

My task consisted in attending meetings until the late hours of the night, taking part in discussions, or lending myself generally along with other Communists in leading the people of the South Side. We debated the housing situation, the best means of forcing the city to authorize open hearings on conditions among Negroes. I gritted my teeth as the daily value of pork chops was tabulated, longing to be at home with my writing. I felt that pork chops were a fundamental item in life, but I preferred that someone else chart their rise and fall in price.

Nealson was cleverer than I and he confronted me before I had a chance to confront him. I was summoned one night to meet Nealson and a "friend." When I arrived at a South Side hotel I was introduced to a short, yellow man who carried himself like Napoleon. He wore glasses, kept his full lips pursed as though he were engaged in perpetual thought. He swaggered when he walked. He spoke slowly, precisely, trying to charge each of his words with more meaning than the words were able to carry. He talked of trivial things in lofty tones. He said that his name was Smith, that he was from Washington, that he planned to launch a national organization among Negroes to federalize all existing Negro institutions so as to achieve a broad unity of action. The three of us sat at a table, facing one another. There were no smiles now. I knew that another and last offer was about to be made to me, and if I did not accept it, there would be open warfare.

"Wright, how would you like to go to Switzerland?" Smith asked with dramatic suddenness.

"I'd like it," I said. "But I'm tied up with work now."

"You can drop that," Nealson said. "This is important."

"What would I do in Switzerland?" I asked.

"You'll go as a youth delegate," Smith said. "From there you can go to the Soviet Union."

"Much as I'd like to, I'm afraid I can't make it," I said honestly. "I simply cannot drop the writing I'm doing now."

We sat looking at one another, smoking silently.

"Has Nealson told you how I feel?" I asked Smith.

Smith did not answer. He stared at me a long time, then spat: "Wright, you're a fool!"

I rose. Smith turned away from me. A breath more of anger and I would have driven my fist into his face. Nealson laughed sheepishly, snorting.

"Was that necessary?" I asked, trembling.

I stood recalling how, in my boyhood, I would have fought until blood ran had anyone said anything like that to me. But I was a man now and master of my rage, able to control the surging emotions. I put on my hat and walked to the door. Keep cool, I said to myself. Don't let this get out of hand . . .

"This is good-bye," I said.

I walked home. My mind was made up. I would attend the next unit meeting and announce my withdrawal, telling the comrades that I still adhered to the ideological program of the party, but that I did not want to be bound any longer by the party's decisions.

I attended the next unit meeting and asked for a place on the agenda, which was readily granted. Nealson was there. Evans was there. Ed Green was there. When my time came to speak, I rose and said:

"Comrades, for the past two years I've worked daily with most of you. Despite this, I have for some time found myself in a difficult position in the party. What has caused this difficulty is a long story which I do not care to recite now; it would serve no purpose. But I tell you honestly that I think I've found a solution of my difficulty. I am proposing here tonight that my membership be dropped from the party rolls. No ideological differences impel me to say this. I simply do not wish to be bound any longer by the party's decisions. I would like to retain my membership in those organizations in which the party has influence, and I shall comply with the party's program in those organizations. I hope that my words will be accepted in the spirit in which they are said. Perhaps sometime in the future I would like to meet and talk with the leaders of the party as to what tasks I can best perform."

I sat down amid a profound silence. The Negro secretary of the meeting looked frightened, glancing at Nealson, Evans, and Ed Green.

"Is there any discussion on Comrade Wright's statement?" the secretary asked finally.

"I move that discussion on Wright's statement be deferred," Nealson said.

A quick vote confirmed Nealson's motion. I looked about the silent room, then reached for my hat and rose.

"I would like to go now," I said.

No one said anything. I walked to the door and out into the night and a heavy burden seemed to lift from my shoulders. I was free. And I had done it in a decent and forthright manner. I had not been bitter. I had not raked up a single recrimination. I had attacked no one. I had disavowed nothing. I remembered, as I walked the night streets, how I had stolen money from the movie house in Jackson, Mississippi; how I had forced the window and had stolen the gun; how I had broken into the college storehouse and had stolen cans of fruit preserves; I remembered how I had lied to my boss man in Memphis when I had wanted to leave my job and come to Chicago; how I had lied to Mr. Hoffman; how I had forged notes to the library in Memphis when I had wanted books to read . . . But I had changed; I had none of that fear, none of those wild impulses now. I had merely confronted my comrades, stated what I felt and had let it go at that.

The Communist party could not say that I was an enemy, that I had attacked them. A Trotskyite or a man bent upon wrecking or disrupting the work of the Communist party would have remained within the organization so as better to quarrel, obstruct. But I had only asked to be free, had accused no one, and had denounced nothing. Perhaps, I told myself, when the Communist party has grown up, when it can work without tactics of terror, threat, invective, intimidation, suspicion, I would go back . . .

Aw, God . . . How naïve I was! I was young and brimming with confidence. I felt that my strength was unlimited. I had neatly solved a problem that had been worrying me for a long time, and now I thought that I could turn my energies to writing and justify myself. I did not know that night how little I understood the political party to which I had belonged. But I soon learned, learned how simple were my motives, how trusting was my attitude, how wide and innocent were my eyes, as round and open and dew-wet as morning-glories . . .

The next night two Negro Communists called at my home. They pretended to be ignorant of what had happened at the unit meeting. Patiently I explained what had occurred.

"Your story does not agree with what Nealson says," they said, revealing the motive of their visit.

"And what does Nealson say?" I asked.

"He says that you are in league with a Trotskyite group, and that you made an appeal for other party members to follow you in leaving the party . . ."

"What?" I gasped. "That's not true. I asked that my membership be dropped. I raised no political issues." What did this mean? I sat pondering. "Look, maybe I ought to make my break with the party clean. If Nealson's going to act this way, I'll resign . . ."

111

"You can't resign," they told me.

"What do you mean?" I demanded.

"No one can resign from the Communist party," they said.

I looked at them and laughed.

"You're talking crazy," I said.

"Nealson would expel you publicly, cut the ground from under your feet if you resigned," they said. "People would think that something was wrong if someone like you quit here on the South Side."

I was angry. Was the party so weak and uncertain of itself that it could not accept what I had said at the unit meeting? Who thought up such tactics? Then, suddenly, I understood. These were the secret, underground tactics of the political movement of the Communists under the czars of Old Russia! The Communist party felt that it had to assassinate me morally merely because I did not want to be bound by its decisions. I saw now that my comrades were acting out a fantasy that had no relation whatever to the reality of their environment.

"Tell Nealson that if he fights me, then, by God, I'll fight him," I said. "If he leaves this damn thing where it is, then all right. If he thinks I won't fight him publicly, he's crazy!"

I was not able to know if my statement reached Nealson, but there was no public outcry against me. But in the ranks of the party itself a storm broke loose and I was branded a traitor, an unstable personality, and one whose faith had failed.

What a weird experience I had had! At no time had I felt at home in the Communist party. I had always felt that the possibility was there, but always I was not quite sure of the motives of the people with whom I worked and they never seemed quite sure of mine. My comrades had known me, my family, my friends; they, God knows, had known my aching poverty. But they had never been able to conquer their fear of the individual way in which I acted and lived, an individuality which life had seared into my blood and bones.

112

I now avoided the comrades as much as possible; and, as I was losing touch with the party, many other young Negroes of the South Side were entering it for the first time. The expansion of the party's activity under the People's Front policy offered many opportunities to young Negroes who, because of race and status, had led cramped lives. The invitation to go to Switzerland as a youth delegate, which I had refused, was accepted by a young Negro who had fought the Communist party and all its ideas until he had seen a chance to take a trip to Europe.

I was transferred by the relief authorities from the South Side Boys' Club to the Federal Negro Theatre to work as a publicity agent. There were days when I was acutely hungry for the incessant analyses that went on among the comrades, but whenever I heard news of the party's inner life, it was of charges and countercharges, reprisals and counterreprisals. I was glad to be out of it. All its energies, it seemed, were absorbed in factional fights, hair-splitting political definitions.

The Federal Negro Theatre, for which I was doing publicity, had run a series of ordinary plays, all of which had been revamped to "Negro style," with jungle scenes, spirituals, and all. For example, the skinny white woman who directed it, an elderly missionary type, would take a play whose characters were white, whose theme dealt with the Middle Ages, and recast it in terms of southern Negro life with overtones of African backgrounds. Contemporary plays dealing realistically with Negro life were spurned as being controversial. There were about forty Negro actors and actresses in the theater, lolling about, yearning, disgruntled, not knowing what to do with themselves.

What a waste of talent, I thought. Here was an opportunity for the production of a worth-while Negro drama and no one was aware of it. I studied the situation, then laid the matter before white friends of mine who held influential positions in the Works Progress Administration. I asked them to replace the white woman—including her quaint aesthetic notions—with someone who knew the Negro and the theater. They promised me that they would act.

Within a month the white woman director had been transferred. We moved from the South Side to the Loop and were housed in a first-rate theater. I successfully recommended Charles DeSheim, a talented Jew, as director. DeSheim and I held long talks during which I outlined what I thought could be accomplished. I urged that our first offering should be a bill of three one-act plays, including Paul Green's *Hymn to the Rising Sun,* a grim, poetical powerful one-acter dealing with chain gang conditions in the South.

I was happy. At last I was in a position to make suggestions and have them acted upon. I was convinced that we had a rare chance to build a genuine Negro theater. I convoked a meeting and introduced DeSheim to the Negro company, telling them that he was a man who knew the theater, who would lead them toward serious dramatics. DeSheim made a speech wherein he said that he was not at the theater to direct it, but to help the Negroes to direct it. He spoke so simply and eloquently that they rose and applauded him.

I then proudly passed out copies of Paul Green's *Hymn to the Rising Sun* to all members of the company. DeSheim assigned reading parts. I sat down to enjoy adult Negro dramatics. But something went wrong. The Negroes stammered and faltered in their lines. Finally they stopped reading altogether. DeSheim looked frightened. One of the Negro actors rose.

"Mr. DeSheim," he began, "we think this play is indecent. We don't want to act in a play like this before the American public. I don't think any such conditions exist in the South. I lived in the South and I never saw any chain gangs. Mr. DeSheim, we want a play that will make the public love us."

I could not believe my ears. I had assumed that the heart of the Negro actor was pining for adult expression in the American theater, that he was ashamed of the stereotypes of clowns, mammies, razors, dice, watermelon, and cotton fields . . . Now they were protesting against dramatic realism! I tried to defend the play and I was heckled down.

"What kind of play do you want?" DeSheim asked them.

They did not know. I went to the office and looked up their records and found that most of them had spent their lives playing cheap vaudeville. I had thought that they played vaudeville because the legitimate theater was barred to them, and now it turned out that they wanted none of the legitimate theater, that they were scared spitless at the prospects of appearing in a play that the public might not like, even though they did not understand that public and had no way of determining its likes or dislikes.

I felt—but only temporarily—that perhaps the whites were right, that Negroes were children and would never grow up. DeSheim informed the company that he would produce any play they liked, and they sat like frightened mice, possessing no words to make known their vague desires.

When I arrived at the theater a few mornings later, I was horrified to find that the company had drawn up a petition demanding the ousting of DeSheim. I was asked to sign the petition and I refused.

"Don't you know your friends?" I asked them.

They glared at me. I called DeSheim to the theater and we went into a frantic conference.

"What must I do?" he asked.

"Take them into your confidence," I said. "Let them know that it is their right to petition for a redress of their grievances."

DeSheim thought my advice sound and, accordingly, he assembled the company and told them that they had a right to petition against him if they wanted to, but that he thought any misunder-

115

standings that existed could be settled smoothly.

"Who told you that we were getting up a petition?" a black man demanded.

DeSheim looked at me and stammered wordlessly.

"There's an Uncle Tom in the theater!" a black girl yelled.

After the meeting a delegation of Negro men came to my office and took out their pocketknives and flashed them in my face.

"You get the hell off this job before we cut your bellybutton out!" they said.

I tried to talk to them, but could not. That day a huge, fat, black woman, a blues singer, found an excuse to pass me as often as possible and she hissed under her breath in a menacing sing-song:

"Lawd, Ah sho hates a white man's nigger."

I telephoned my white friends in the Works Progress Administration:

"Transfer me at once to another job, or I'll be murdered."

Within twenty-four hours DeSheim and I were given our papers. We shook hands and went our separate ways.

I was transferred to a white experimental theatrical company as a publicity agent and I resolved to keep my ideas to myself, or, better, to write them down and not attempt to translate them into reality. I dodged the Negro theatrical world and kept rigorously clear of all members of the Communist party. Whenever I met any of my erstwhile comrades, they refused to acknowledge my existence in accordance with a party principle that made it imperative that all "traitors be isolated from the working class."

One evening a group of Negro Communists called at my home and asked to speak to me in strict secrecy. I took them into my room and locked the door.

"Dick," they began abruptly, "the party wants you to attend a meeting Sunday."

"Why?" I asked. "I'm no longer a member."

"That's all right. They want you to be present," they said.

"Communists don't speak to me on the street," I said. "Now, why do you want me at a meeting?"

They hedged. They did not want to tell me.

"If you can't tell me, then I can't come," I said.

They whispered among themselves and finally decided to take me into their confidence.

"Dick, Ross is going to be tried," they said.

"For what?"

They recited a long list of political offenses of which they alleged that he was guilty.

"But what has this got to do with me?"

"If you come, you'll find out," they said.

"I'm not that naïve," I said, smiling. I was suspicious now. Were they trying to lure me to a trial and expel me? "This trial might turn out to be mine . . ."

They swore that they had no intention of placing me on trial, that the party merely wanted me to observe Ross's trial so that I might learn what happened to "enemies of the working class."

"But I'm not your enemy," I said.

"We want to save you," they said.

"Save me from what?" I asked. "I'm not lost."

"We have your welfare at heart," they said.

"Then why did you-all lie and call me a Trotskyite?"

"Nealson lost his head," they said. "When you left the party, he had to hit at you some way."

"Why do you spend your time in these crazy witch hunts?" I asked them. "You claim to be fighting oppression, but you spend more of your time fighting each other than in fighting your avowed enemies." As I spoke to them I recalled the time when my mother had slapped me when I had asked her—in the far-off days of Arkansas—why my "uncle" had run away from the white people, why he had not fought back; my mother had given me a ringing slap—fear had made her do it. And I felt that it was the fear of their enemies that made Communists—unconsciously compensating for their fear—fight one another so doggedly and persistently. But I did not tell them that; they would not have understood. "Look, Ross is a minor street agitator. Forget him. And in two weeks he'd be no issue at all."

"We're going to make an example out of Ross," they told me. "His trial will be an education for the working class, and for you, too, if you'll come."

As they talked, my old love of witnessing something new came over me. I wanted to see this trial, but I did not want to risk being placed on trial myself.

"Listen," I told them. "I'm not guilty of Nealson's charges. If I showed up at this trial, it would seem that I am."

"No, it won't. Please come."

"All right. But, listen . . . If I'm tricked, I'll fight. You hear? I don't trust Nealson. I'm not a politician and I cannot anticipate all the funny moves of a man who spends his waking hours plotting."

Ross's trial took place that following Sunday afternoon. Comrades stood inconspicuously on guard about the meeting hall, at the doors, down the street, and along the hallways. When I appeared, I was ushered in quickly. I was tense. It was a rule that once you had entered a meeting of this kind you could not leave until the meeting was over; it was feared that you might go to the police and denounce them all.

Acting upon the loftiest of impulses, filled with love for those who suffer, urged toward fellowship with the rebellious, committed to sacrifice, why was it that there existed among Communists so much hate, suspicion, bitterness, and internecine strife? I stood in the midst of people I loved and I was afraid of them. I felt profoundly that they were traveling in the right direction, yet if their having power to rule had depended merely upon my lifting my right hand, I would have been afraid to do so. My heart throbbed and I whispered to myself: God, I love these people, but I'm glad that they're not in power, or they'd shoot me!

No one spoke to me. Some of the party leaders shot me hostile glances and looked away. Why had I been called in to witness this trial? I sat with jumpy nerves, impatient for the trial to get under way. Despite my fear, I was keenly curious. But I was determined not to participate in any way, for that would have surely, by implication, incriminated me in a network of guilt which I did not share.

Ross, the accused, sat alone at a table in the front of the hall, his face distraught. I felt sorry for him, yet I could not escape feeling that he enjoyed this. For him, this was perhaps the highlight of an otherwise bleak existence.

I was for these people. Being a Negro, I could not help it. They did not hate Negroes. They had no racial prejudices. Many of the white men in the hall were married to Negro women, and many of the Negro men were married to white women. Jews, Germans, Russians, Spaniards, all races and nationalities were represented without any distinctions whatever.

Racial hate had been the bane of my life, and here before my eyes was concrete proof that it could be abolished. Yet a new hate had come to take the place of the rankling racial hate. It was irrational that Communists should hate what they called "intellectuals," or anybody who tried to think for himself. I had fled men who did not like the color of my skin, and now I was among men who did not like the tone of my thoughts.

In trying to grasp why Communists hated intellectuals, my mind was led back again to the accounts I had read of the Russian Revolution. There had existed in Old Russia millions of poor, ignorant people who were exploited by a few, educated, arrogant noblemen, and it became natural for the Russian Communists to

119

associate betrayal with intellectualism. But there existed in the Western world an element that baffled and frightened the Communist party: the prevalence of self-achieved literacy. Even a Negro, entrapped by ignorance and exploitation—as I had been —could, if he had the will and the love for it, learn to read and understand the world in which he lived. And it was these people that the Communists could not understand. The American Communists, enjoying legality, were using the methods forged by the underground Russian Bolshevik fire, and therefore had to have their followers willing to accept all explanations of reality, even when the actual situation did not call for it.

The heritage of free thought,—which no man could escape if he read at all,—the spirit of the Protestant ethic which one suckled, figuratively, with one's mother's milk, that self-generating energy that made a man feel, whether he realized it or not, that he had to work and redeem himself through his own acts, all this was forbidden, taboo. And yet this was the essence of that cultural heritage which the Communist party had sworn to carry forward, whole and intact, into the future. But the Communist party did not recognize the values that it had sworn to save when it saw them; the slightest sign of any independence of thought or feeling, even if it aided the party in its work, was enough to make one suspect, to brand one as a dangerous traitor.

The trial began in a quiet, informal manner. The comrades acted like a group of neighbors sitting in judgment upon one of their kind who had stolen a chicken. Anybody could ask and get the floor. There was absolute freedom of speech. Yet the meeting had an amazingly formal structure of its own, a structure that went as deep as the desire of men to live together.

A member of the Central Committee of the Communist party rose and gave a description of the world situation. He spoke without emotion and piled up hard facts. He painted a horrible but masterful picture of Fascism's aggression in Germany, Italy, and Japan.

I accepted the reason why the trial began in this manner. It was imperative that there be postulated against what or whom Ross's crimes had been committed. Therefore there had to be established in the minds of all present a vivid picture of mankind under oppression. And it was a true picture. Perhaps no organization on earth, save the Communist party, possessed so detailed a knowledge of how workers lived, for its sources of information stemmed directly from the workers themselves.

The next speaker discussed the role of the Soviet Union as the world's lone workers' state, how the Soviet Union was hemmed in by enemies, how the Soviet Union was trying to industrialize itself, what sacrifices she was making to help the workers of the world to steer a path toward peace through the idea of collective security.

The facts presented so far were as true as any facts could be in this uncertain world. Yet not one word had been said of the accused, who sat listening like any other member. The time had not yet come to include him and his crimes in this picture of global struggle. An absolute had first to be established in the minds of the comrades so that they could measure the success or failure of their deeds by it. There was no mysticism, no invoking of God, merely a passionate identification of all present with a will to right wrongs. It was a simple, elemental morality. Communism had found a moral code that could control the conduct of men, yet it was a code that stemmed from practical living, and not from the injunctions of the supernatural.

Still another speaker rose and described the domestic situation in the United States and linked it with the world scene. This was done in a leisurely, painstaking manner; yet the people in the hall were charged with passion; a sense of human destiny lived; an atmosphere of human frailty was present.

Finally a speaker came forward and spoke of Chicago's South Side, its Negro population, their sufferings and handicaps, linking all that, also, to the world struggle. Then still another speaker followed and described the tasks of the Communist party of the South Side. At last, the world, the national, and the local pictures had been fused into one overwhelming drama of moral struggle in which everybody in the hall was participating. This presentation had lasted for more than three hours, but it had enthroned a new sense of reality in the hearts of those present, a sense of man on earth. With the exception of the church and its myths and legends, there was no agency in the world so capable of making men feel the earth and the people upon it as the Communist party.

I knew, as I watched, that I was looking at the future of mankind, that this way of living would finally win out. I knew that in no other way could the emotional capacities, the passional nature of men be so deeply tapped. In no other system yet devised could man so clearly reveal his destiny on earth, a destiny to rise and grapple with the world in which he lives, to wring from it the satisfactions he feels he must have. I knew, as I watched and listened, that but few people understood the essence of Communism, its passional dynamics; but a few knew that Communism was more important than any of its individual parties, than the sum of all its tactics, strategies, theories, mistakes, and tragedies. I knew that once this system became entrenched on earth, for good or bad, it could not fail, that all Europe and her armies could not destroy the Soviet Union, that the spirit of self-sacrifice that Communism engendered in men would astound the world.

And these people had asked me to come and listen to another man being tried so that I might know what was in store for me if I went wrong. I was with them. Could I not rise up and tell them? But, even as I thought of it, I knew they would not be able to know when I was telling the truth. My kind of helping was something frightening to them. If I talked, I would only incriminate myself further.

I had wanted to tell others what these men felt. I understood their impulses, the long years' privation and hurt out of which they had come to Communism. I knew that I did not know as much politics as Buddy Nealson, as the members of the Central Committee, or the members of the Communist International. Politics was not my game; the human heart was my game, but it was only in the realm of politics that I could see the depths of the human heart. I had wanted to make others see what was in the Communist heart, what the Communists were after; but I was on trial by proxy, condemned by them.

Toward evening the direct charges against Ross were made, not by the leaders of the party but by Ross's friends, those who knew him best! It was crushing. Ross wilted. His emotions could not withstand the weight of the moral pressure. No one was terrorized into giving information against him. They gave it willingly, citing dates, conversations, scenes. The black mass of Ross's wrongdoing emerged slowly and irrefutably. He could not deny it. No one could.

They did not place me on trial because they did not know how to give names to what they feared in me. I had not fought them as Ross had; I had not challenged a single policy of theirs. It was my way of thinking and feeling that they feared. The conditions under which I had to work were what baffled them. Writing had to be done in loneliness and Communism had declared war upon human loneliness. Alone, they said, a man was weak; united with others, he was strong. Therefore they habitually feared a man who stood alone. Communism spelt the unity of human life, and when a Communist, newly risen from his oppressed isolation and feeling strange and lonely because of it, saw another man seeking seclusion, he became afraid of him. The Communism I looked upon was impatient of extended processes, of results that could not be obtained overnight, of an act that could not be performed within a day. This was how America had embraced Communism; this was America's first green fruit of materialistic rebellion.

The moment came for Ross to defend himself. I had been told that he had arranged for friends of his to testify in his behalf, but he called upon no one. He stood, trembling; he tried to talk and his words would not come. The hall was as still as death. Guilt was written in every pore of his black skin. His hands shook. He held onto the edge of the table to keep on his feet. His personality, his sense of himself, had been obliterated. Yet he could not have been so humbled unless he had shared and accepted the vision that had crushed him, the common vision that bound us all together.

"Comrades," he said in a low, charged voice, "I'm guilty of all the charges, all of them . . ."

His voice broke in a sob. No one prodded him. No one tortured him. No one threatened him. He was free to go out of the hall and never see another Communist. But he did not want to. He could not. The vision of a communal world had sunk down into his soul and it would never leave him until life left him. He talked on, outlining how he had erred, how he would reform.

I knew, as I sat there, that there were many people who thought they knew life who had been skeptical of the Moscow trials. But they could not have been skeptical had they witnessed this astonishing trial. Ross had not been doped; he had been awakened. It was not a fear of the Communist party that had made him confess, but a fear of the punishment that he would exact of himself that made him tell of his wrongdoings. The Communists had talked to him until they had given him new eyes with which to see his own crime. And then they sat back and listened to him tell how he had erred. He was one with all the members there, regardless of race or color; his heart was theirs and their hearts were his; and when a man reaches that state of kinship with others, that degree of oneness, or when a trial has made him kin after he has been sundered from them by wrongdoing, then he must rise and say, out of a sense of the deepest morality in the world:

124

"I'm guilty. Forgive me."

This, to me, was a spectacle of glory; and yet, because it had condemned me, because it was blind and ignorant, I felt that it was a spectacle of horror. The blindness of their limited lives—lives truncated and impoverished by the oppression they had suffered long before they had ever heard of Communism—made them think that I was with their enemies. American life had so corrupted their consciousness that they were unable to recognize their friends when they saw them. I knew that if they had held state power I would have been declared guilty of treason and my execution would have followed. And I knew that they felt, with all the strength of their black blindness, that they were right.

I could not stay until the end. I was anxious to get out of the hall and into the streets and shake free from the gigantic tension that had hold of me. I rose and went to the door; a comrade shook his head, warning me that I could not leave until the trial had ended.

"You can't leave now," he said.

"I'm going out of here," I said, my anger making my voice sound louder than I intended.

We glared at each other. Another comrade came running up. I stepped forward. The comrade who had rushed up gave the signal for me to be allowed to leave. They did not want violence, and neither did I. They stepped aside.

I went into the dark Chicago streets and walked home through the cold, filled with a sense of sadness. Once again I told myself that I must learn to stand alone. I did not feel so wounded by their rejection of me that I wanted to spend my days bleating about what they had done. Perhaps what I had already learned to feel in my childhood saved me from that futile path. I lay in bed that night and said to myself: I'll be for them, even though they are not for me.

The next morning a Negro Communist came to my house

before I was out of bed. He sat and would not look at me.

"What do you want, Harold?" I asked.

"I don't know how to say what I want to say," he said.

"Say it anyhow. I can stand anything now."

"Gee, I'm sorrier than I've ever been in all my life," he cried. "I didn't know what they were going to do . . ."

"Do you mean that?" I asked.

"God, yes!"

"Thanks. I'm no enemy of the party."

"It was horrible," he said.

"There was a glimpse of glory in it, too," I said.

"What?"

"Nothing," I said.

He left. He was the only Communist who had enough courage to speak to me.

# Chapter VI

F ROM the Federal Experimental Theater I was transferred to
the Federal Writers' Project, and I tried to earn my bread
by writing guidebooks. Many of the writers on the project were
members of the Communist party and they kept their revolutionary vows that restrained them from speaking to "traitors of the
working class." I sat beside them in the office, ate next to them
in restaurants, and rode up and down in the elevators with them,
but they always looked straight ahead, wordlessly.

After working on the project for a few months, I was made
acting supervisor of essays and straightway I ran into political
difficulties. One morning the administrator of the project called
me into his office.

"Wright, who are your friends on this project?" he asked.

"I don't know," I said. "Why?"

"Well, you ought to find out soon," he said.

"What do you mean?"

"Some people are asking for your removal on the grounds that
you are incompetent," he said.

"Who are they?"

He named several of my erstwhile comrades. Yes, it had come
to that. They were trying to take the bread out of my mouth, and
I agreed with them too much to want to fight back.

"What do you propose to do about their complaints?" I asked.

"Nothing," he said, laughing. "I think I understand what's

happening here. I'm not going to let them drive you off this job."

I thanked him and rose to go to the door. Something in his words had not sounded right. I turned and faced him.

"*This* job?" I repeated. "What do you mean?"

"You mean to say that you don't know?" he asked.

"Know what? What are you talking about?"

"Why did you leave the Federal Negro Theater?"

"I had trouble there. They drove me off the job, the Negroes did."

"And you don't think that they had any encouragement?" he asked me ironically.

I sat again. This was deadly. I gaped at him.

"You needn't fear here," he said. "You work, write . . ."

"It's hard to believe that," I murmured.

"Forget it," he said.

I returned to my desk and stared at the Communists who sat near me. I was not angry. I was sorry. How far can they go acting like this? I wondered. I knew that if they had succeeded in getting me fired they would have considered it a triumph of proletarian tactics. Why could they not forget me? I was opposing no policy of theirs. I was not speaking or writing against them. But the worst was yet to come.

One day at noon I closed my desk and went down in the elevator. When I reached the first floor of the building, I saw a picket line moving to and fro in the streets. Many of the men and women carrying placards were old friends of mine, and they were chanting for higher wages for Works Progress Administration artists and writers. It was not the kind of picket line that one was not supposed to cross, and as I started away from the door I heard my name shouted:

"There's Wright, that goddamn Trotskyite!"

"That sonofabitch Wright is with 'em, too!"

"We know you, you bastard!"

"Wright's a traitor, too!"

For a moment it seemed that I ceased to live. I had now reached that point where I was cursed aloud in the busy streets of America's second largest city. It shook me as nothing else had.

I decided upon a bold, open, and friendly move. I had to put a stop to this hounding of me. I would go directly to the head of the local Communist party and have it out with him, talk to him, explain things. I implored a friend of mine to use what influence he had to obtain an appointment for me with the secretary of the party.

Weeks passed and finally word came that I had an appointment, not with the secretary, but with the secretary's secretary, a girl, Alma Zetkin. I sighed and accepted it.

When I walked into the headquarters of the Communist party, I was ushered into Alma Zetkin's presence. She was plump, blonde, blue-eyed, with big braids of hair circling her head. She was shuffling a pile of papers in her hand. She did not look up.

"I've an appointment to see you," I said. "But I'd like to see Bernard, the party secretary."

"What do you want with him?" she asked, not lifting her head, her eyes glued to the papers in her hand.

"I want to discuss my party affiliation with him," I said.

"He cannot see you about such matters," she said.

"With whom can I talk?"

"I can listen to what you have to say," she said.

She was cold, distant; I knew that she had already made up her mind, that a decision had already been made about me.

"There're a lot of misunderstandings that I'd like to clear up," I said, forcing the words out of me, for I knew now that my errand was futile.

"What are they?" she asked, still not looking at me.

Quietly I outlined the story, sticking to bare facts, feeling that I was talking to a stone wall. When I had finished, she said:

"We can't help you with that problem."

"What do you mean?"

"If you can't get along with your comrades on the South Side, what do you expect us to do about it?" she snapped, her eyes flashing blue and cold and hard.

"They're not people with whom one can talk," I said. "I'm called a Trotskyite. WHY?"

"Are you a Trotskyite?" she asked, looking at me full now.

"No, and why would you think I was one?" I asked.

She laughed silently and turned to her papers again.

"Well, what have you to say?" I asked.

"There's nothing we can do for you here," she said.

I stood silent for a moment. I had had my answer. Yet the answer did not seem sensible, intelligible. I had not solved anything. I looked at her; she was still intent upon the papers.

"Good-bye," I said, turning and walking toward the door.

She did not answer. I paused at the door and stared at her again; she was still gazing at the papers. I went out.

That night I tossed sleepless, trying to imagine what had been in Alma Zetkin's mind, what she had been told, what were her motives. And my mind could find nothing but improbable answers. Had she been warned that I must under no circumstances be given encouragement? If so, why? Even Ross, who had actively fought the party within the ranks of the party, was still a member in good standing. But I, whom they had officially accused of nothing, was an open enemy in their eyes.

Nothing that I could think of could explain the reality I saw. My mind was like an ulcer whenever it touched upon what had happened to my relations with the party. I asked myself why a million times, and there were no answers.

Days passed. I continued on my job, where I functioned as the shop chairman of the union which I had helped to organize, though my election as shop chairman had been bitterly opposed by the party. In their efforts to nullify my influence in the union, my old comrades were willing to kill the union itself.

As May Day of 1936 approached, it was voted by the union membership that we should march in the public procession. On the morning of May Day I received printed instructions as to the time and place where our union contingent would assemble to join the parade. At noon I hurried to the spot and found that the parade was already in progress. In vain I searched for the banners of my union local. Where were they? I went up and down the streets, asking for the location of my local.

"Oh, that local's gone fifteen minutes ago," a Negro told me. "If you're going to march, you'd better fall in somewhere."

I thanked him and walked through the milling crowds. Suddenly I heard my name called. I turned. To my left was the Communist party's South Side section, lined up and ready to march.

"Come here!" an old party friend called me.

I walked over to him.

"Aren't you marching today?" he asked me.

"I missed my union local," I told him.

"What the hell," he said. "March with us."

"I don't know," I said, remembering my last visit to the headquarters of the party, and my status as an "enemy."

"This is May Day," he said. "Get into the ranks."

"You know the trouble I've had," I said.

"That's nothing," he said. "Everybody's marching today."

"I don't think I'd better," I said, shaking my head.

"Goddamn, are you scared?" he asked. "This is *May Day.*"

He caught my right arm and pulled me into line beside him. I stood talking to him, asking him about his work, about common friends.

"Get out of our ranks!" a voice barked in my ears.

I turned. A white Communist, a leader of the district of the Communist party, Cy Perry, a slender, close-cropped fellow, stood glaring at me.

"I . . . It's May Day and I want to march," I said.

"Get out!" he shouted.

"I was invited here," I said.

I turned to the Negro Communist who had invited me into the ranks. I did not want public violence. I looked at my friend. He turned his eyes away. He was afraid. I did not know what to do.

"You asked me to march here," I said to him.

He did not answer.

"Tell him that you did invite me," I said, pulling his sleeve.

"I'm asking you for the last time to get out of our ranks!" Cy Perry shouted.

I did not move. I had intended to, but I was beset by so many impulses that I could not act. Another white Communist came to assist Perry. Perry caught hold of my collar and pulled at me. I resisted. They held me fast. I struggled to free myself.

"Turn me loose!" I said.

Hands lifted me bodily from the sidewalk; I felt myself being pitched headlong through the air. I saved myself from landing on my head by clutching a curbstone with my hands. Slowly I rose and stood. Perry and his assistant were glaring at me. The rows of white and black Communists were looking at me with cold eyes of nonrecognition. I could not quite believe what had happened, even though my hands were smarting and bleeding. I had suffered a public, physical assault by two white Communists with black Communists looking on. I could not move from the spot. I was empty of any idea about what to do. But I did not feel belligerent. I had outgrown my childhood. I did not know how much time elapsed as I stood there, numb, astonished; but, suddenly, the vast ranks of the Communist party began to move. Scarlet banners with the hammer and sickle emblem of world revolution were lifted, and they fluttered in the May breeze. Drums beat. Voices were chanting. The tramp of many feet shook the earth. A long line of set-faced men and women, white and black, flowed past me.

I followed the procession to the Loop and went into Grant Park Plaza and sat upon a bench. I was not thinking; I could not think. But an objectivity of vision was being born within me. A surging sweep of many odds and ends came together and formed an attitude, a perspective. They're blind, I said to myself. Their enemies have blinded them with too much oppression. I lit a cigarette and I heard a song floating out over the sunlit air.

*Arise, you pris'ners of starvation!*

I remembered the stories I had written, the stories in which I had assigned a role of honor and glory to the Communist party and I was glad that they were down in black and white, were finished. For I knew in my heart that I would never be able to write that way again, would never be able to feel with that simple sharpness about life, would never again express such passionate hope, would never again make so total a commitment of faith.

*Arise, you wretched of the earth . . .*

The days of my past, of my youth, were receding from me like a rolling tide, leaving me alone upon high, dry ground, leaving me with a quieter and deeper consciousness.

*For justice thunders condemnation . . .*

My thoughts seemed to be coming from somewhere within me, as by a power of their own: It's going to take a long and bloody time, a lot of stumbling and a lot of falling, before they find the right road.

They will have to grope about blindly in the sunshine, butting their heads against every mistake, bruising their bodies against

133

every illusion, making a million futile errors and suffering for them, bleeding for them, until they learn how to live, I thought.

Somehow man had been sundered from man and, in his search for a new unity, for a new wholeness, for oneness again, he would have to blunder into a million walls to find merely that he could not go in certain directions. No one could tell him. He would have to learn by marching down history's bloody road. He would have to purchase his wisdom of life with sacred death. He would have to pay dearly to learn just a little.

But perhaps that is the way it has always been with man . . .

*A better world's in birth . . .*

The procession still passed. Banners still floated. Voices of hope still chanted.

I headed toward home alone, really alone now, telling myself that in all the sprawling immensity of our mighty continent the least-known factor of living was the human heart, the least-sought goal of being was a way to live a human life. Perhaps, I thought, out of my tortured feelings I could fling a spark into this darkness. I would try, not because I wanted to but because I felt that I had to if I were to live at all.

I sat alone in my narrow room, watching the sun sink slowly in the chilly May sky. I was restless. I rose to get my hat; I wanted to visit some friends and tell them what I felt, to talk. Then I sat down. Why do that? My problem was here, here with me, here in this room, and I would solve it here alone or not at all. Yet, I did not want to face it; it frightened me. I rose again and went out into the streets. Halfway down the block I stopped, undecided. Go back . . . I returned to my room and sat again, determined to look squarely at my life.

Well, what had I got out of living in the city? What had I got out of living in the South? What had I got out of living in America? I paced the floor, knowing that all I possessed were words and a dim knowledge that my country had shown me no examples of how to live a human life. All my life I had been full of a hunger for a new way to live . . .

I heard a trolley lumbering past over steel tracks in the early dusk and I knew that underpaid, bewildered black men and women were returning to their homes from serving their white masters. In the front room of my apartment our radio was playing, pouring a white man's voice into my home, a voice that hinted of a coming war that would consume millions of lives.

Yes, the whites were as miserable as their black victims, I thought. If this country can't find its way to a human path, if it can't inform conduct with a deep sense of life, then all of us, black as well as white, are going down the same drain . . .

I picked up a pencil and held it over a sheet of white paper, but my feelings stood in the way of my words. Well, I would wait, day and night, until I knew what to say. Humbly now, with no vaulting dream of achieving a vast unity, I wanted to try to build a bridge of words between me and that world outside, that world which was so distant and elusive that it seemed unreal.

I would hurl words into this darkness and wait for an echo, and if an echo sounded, no matter how faintly, I would send other words to tell, to march, to fight, to create a sense of the hunger for life that gnaws in us all, to keep alive in our hearts a sense of the inexpressibly human.

# Afterword

When *Black Boy* was published by Harper & Brothers in March 1945 and offered as a selection of the Book-of-the-Month Club, American reviewers responded almost unanimously with enthusiasm. Four years earlier, *Native Son* had shocked an audience not yet prepared to look beyond the mask of the smiling Negro to discover his hatred and his desire for revenge against white racism. With that book Wright's reputation as a critic of the American system and as a tough, violent muckraking novelist was established. By the close of World War II, however, racial issues were more often being aired by blacks in terms of the "double victory" campaign—discrimination in weapons factories was attacked by a march on Washington organized by A. Philip Randolph; segregation in the Red Cross blood banks raised vigorous protest in the black press. From Sinclair Lewis' *Kingsblood Royal* and Lillian Smith's *Strange Fruit* to Howard Fast's more radical *Freedom Road,* a spate of books dealing with what was now being called "the American dilemma" succeeded, in fiction at least, in showing the concern of well-meaning whites.

*Black Boy* was a striking achievement: few of its predecessors had exemplified such power and sincerity. Moreover, the quality of Wright's writing was high. Attacking as it did the blunting effect of racial oppression on Southern childhood, the book could not help but emphasize black resilience and courage as embodied in the author. It thus corresponded to the very American type of success story characteristic of slave narratives—the journey from

136

hard times to freedom, if not exactly from rags to riches. Its success, we can surmise, rested as much on the assertion of a self-realization as on the distinctive character of Wright's talent and artistic struggle. He himself had wanted his story to stand as a pattern of black survival and he had accepted the onus of becoming a spokesman out of a deep sense of ethnic solidarity. In an interview granted to *PM Magazine* on April 14, 1945, he stated:

I wanted to give, lend my tongue to the voiceless Negro boys. I feel that way about the deprived Negro children of the South: "Not until the sun ceases to shine on you shall I disown you."

At the same time, Wright was also attempting to re-create his growth as a writer and a politically conscious citizen who often found himself at odds with the national culture. His writing had already evinced a clearly autobiographical quality in such early pieces as the bitterly satirical "Ethics of Living Jim Crow," the more humorous vignette "What You Don't Know Won't Hurt You," and in some episodes of *Uncle Tom's Children* and *Native Son*. As early as 1940, Wright had been told by his agent and friend Paul Reynolds that he should write his autobiography, but he had asked for time to consider this suggestion. Now, finally, at the age of thirty-five, he was convinced of the value and necessity of delving into his own past. A lecture about his formative years which he gave at Fisk University in 1942 created such a liberating explosion of enthusiasm among the blacks and one of such angry resentment among the whites in the audience that Wright realized: "I had accidentally blundered into the secret black, hidden core of race relations in the United States. That core is this: nobody is ever expected to speak honestly about the problem." He had, no doubt, the exemplary function of the book in mind all the time, and he was fond of repeating: "One of the things that made me write is that I realize that I am a very average Negro. Maybe that's what

137

makes me extraordinary." However, the therapeutic role of plunging into his past, of dealing with embarrassing sexual incidents, traumas, and moral dilemmas, and of trying to focus his approach in such a way as to preserve the balance necessary for truthfulness was probably the most beneficial result for the author himself. This is suggested in his description of "The Birth of *Black Boy,*" which appeared in the New York *Post* on November 30, 1944:

The real hard terror of writing like this came when I found that writing of one's life was vastly different from speaking of it. I was rendering a close and emotionally connected account of my experience and the ease I had had in speaking from notes at Fisk would not come again. I found that to tell the truth is the hardest thing on earth, harder than fighting in a war, harder than taking part in a revolution. If you try it you will find that at times sweat will break upon you. You will find that even if you succeed in discounting the attitudes of others to you and your life, you must wrestle with yourself most of all, fight with yourself; for there will surge up in you a strong desire to alter facts, to dress up your feelings. You'll find that there are many things that you don't want to admit about yourself and others. As your record shapes itself an awed wonder haunts you. And yet there is no more exciting an adventure than trying to be honest in this way. The clean, strong feeling that sweeps you when you've done it makes you know that.

Wright's nearly psychoanalytical explanations for his own motives, which run like an unabating burden throughout the autobiography, are the clear recognition of the power and weight of one's past. His explanatory comment does not really blend with the story's dialogue, its descriptions, its action, or its lyrical outbursts; it is a reflexive voice which enables the reader to gauge the passage of the author's life and the ensuing change in his perspective. It constitutes a meditation on Wright's growth from his Mississippi environment in the 1910s, when he had his first recollections, to setting them down on paper in New York in the mid-1940s. This sense of Wright's having reached a degree of success is essential to the reader because it enables him to look back from a given point of achievement in order to pass judgment on the obstacles conquered and on the perseverance and energy needed in the process. The sense of exhilaration associated with consolidation and growth is most strongly communicated in the conclusion of *Black Boy*, where Wright capsulizes his Southern ordeals and wonders about his future:

I was taking a part of the South to transplant in alien soil, to see if it could grow differently, if it could drink of new and cool rains, bend in strange winds, respond to the warmth of other suns, and, perhaps, to bloom. . . . I headed North, full of a hazy notion that life could be lived with dignity, that the personalities of others should not be violated, that men should be able to confront other men without fear or shame, and that if men were lucky in their living on earth they might win some redeeming meaning for their having struggled and suffered here beneath the stars.

It should be pointed out that this final paragraph of *Black Boy* represents little more than a statement of aims, a nearly mystical expression of hopeful potentialities. When Wright muses that the novelist's personality will be allowed "perhaps to bloom" in Chicago, the reader is tempted to focus on the blossoming and to overlook the emphasis on the mere *possibility* of such realization. Thus one can jump a little too readily to the conclusion that Wright, who certainly deserved whatever luck he had, finally found in the United States the kind of soil where his blackness could bloom, where his racial suffering could be redeemed. Such an optimistic reading of the novelist's flight to Chicago is definitely influenced by the knowledge that Wright had, by 1945, established his reputation as the leading Afro-American novelist. In this light, the very success of *Black Boy* as a best seller is taken to demonstrate the soundness of whatever optimism lies in

Wright's "hazy notions" of a better environment. *Black Boy* is commonly construed as a typical success story, and thus it has been used by the American liberal to justify his own optimism regarding his country.

It is true that Wright did stress the appeal of the North, developing the dream of escape to a better land, which had sustained generations of fugitive slaves on their way to Canaan. It is equally true that Wright, because he placed his autobiography in the literary tradition of slave narratives, expressed hopes so powerful that one might easily overlook the depth of the disappointments he was to experience. Yet when Wright reflects upon his Chicago experience in *American Hunger*, his perspective is in fact extremely critical of the American system as a whole. Superimposed on the spectrum of his fiction, this latter section of his autobiography evokes a range of human possibilities restricted to the ludicrous shallowness of Jake Jackson caught in the squirrel cage of *Lawd Today* or the dramatic horror of Bigger Thomas' violent fate.

The opening pages of *American Hunger* describe the complete unpreparedness of the Southern migrants who came up to flood the Midwest metropolis. Through scattered references to his family and their inability to respond to his needs, Wright makes clear his own uprootedness, his loneliness among the black masses whose struggle he had already evoked in *Twelve Million Black Voices:* "We were barely born as a folk when we headed for the tall and sprawling centers of steel and stone. . . ." That is the tragedy of black migration. Turned loose to fend for themselves, such youngsters as Wright were likely to turn into "bad guys" or complacent do-nothings. The conditions of life in an urban neighborhood, overcrowded and decaying from the outset, made rural folk culture, previously a sustaining force, largely irrelevant. And finally it crumbled in face of the materialistic survival values of city life, injecting Wright and others like him with a sense of solitude among their own people. For Wright, such loneliness resulted as well from his inability to participate in the unsophisticated life around him and to lose himself in such anaesthetic diversions as Saturday-night wenching and carousing. He was, moreover, frustrated by the realization that mass civilization, as it had been established in the United States, had nothing enduring to offer:

Everything seemed makeshift, temporary. I caught an abiding sense of insecurity in the personalities of the people around me. . . . Wherever my eyes turned they saw stricken, frightened black faces trying vainly to cope with a civilization that they did not understand.

Indeed, white people suffered just as much from alienation. Of the white waitresses with whom he worked in a restaurant, Wright remarked:

They were an eager, restless, talkative, ignorant bunch, but casually kind and impersonal for all that. They knew nothing of hate and fear, and strove instinctively to avoid all passion. . . . Their constant outward-looking, their mania for radios, cars, and a thousand other trinkets made them dream and fix their eyes upon the trash of life. . . . Perhaps it would be possible for the Negro to become reconciled to his plight if he could be made to believe that his sufferings were for some remote, high, sacrificial end; but sharing the culture that condemns him, and seeing that a lust for trash is what blinds the nation to his claims, is what sets storms to rolling in his soul.

Wright's sentiments here are far from those in the potentially rosy ending of *Black Boy. American Hunger* in no way lends itself to being interpreted as a success story. In fact, the complete original version of Wright's autobiography ("Black Boy" plus "American Hunger") takes him not only to the Middle West in 1927 but to the hectic heart of New York City in 1937 with no increase in his general satisfaction. Not only does it range further than *Black Boy* alone, showing Wright's tempering and emergence as a left-wing writer; it also provides a much fuller picture of American life. The stunting experiences suffered in *Black Boy* are followed by more overtly disturbing occurrences in the North; *American Hunger* represents the culmination of Wright's disappointment. While *Black Boy* is illuminated by a quotation from Job stressing the blindness of racism, the epigraph to *American Hunger* raises the question of the basic sanity of the American system through a lightly ironic folk verse: "Sometimes I wonder, huh/Wonder if other people wonder, huh,/Just like I do, oh, my Lord, just like I do."

It was only at the time of the decision to publish the first section of the autobiography separately that the five present concluding pages of *Black Boy* were added. These new pages allow a rather more optimistic interpretation than the original rather sober ending, which they now follow: "This was the culture from which I sprang. This was the terror from which I fled." The second part ended, as it still does, with Wright's desperate attempt, after his failure to work hand in hand with the Communists, to raise an echo by hurling his words to the world. Wright's original title for the section, "The Horror and the Glory," which may apply to the policies of the C.P.U.S.A. as well as to the fluctuating conditions of life during the Depression, is far from hopeful. Thus, the final pages of the entire autobiography, instead of pointing, as does *Black Boy,* to Wright's success as a writer and to his achievement as a black American, actually extended his argument into the existential quandary of a politically conscious human being confronted with a barren social and spiritual horizon.

One may indeed wonder how Wright allowed *Black Boy* to be published as it finally was in the spring of 1945, since the two-part work—*Black Boy* plus *American Hunger*—seems better to correspond to his original aim. It is necessary to recall the genesis of the book in late 1942. For some time, Wright kept unusually silent about it, although he commented freely on the progress of another work, a novel about domestic workers, which he was eventually to discard. On December 17, 1943, he sent his manuscript to Paul Reynolds with a terse and surprisingly unsure comment:

Here is another manuscript, the value of which I do not know. Read it and if it is worth showing to Harper's, then let them see it; if, however, you think that such a book ought not to be published by me at this time, then hold it. I don't think that there is much that I will ever be able to do on this script. Perhaps a section or two here and there will have to be pulled out. But, on the whole, the thing will have to stand as it is, for better or worse.

I called it *American Hunger,* but later I thought that *Black Hunger* would be a better title.*

Reynolds reacted enthusiastically. Edward Aswell, Wright's editor at Harper's and his well-heeded friendly adviser, accepted the book at once and scheduled its publication for the fall of 1944. It was Aswell who suggested the subtitle "The Biography of a Courageous Negro," to which Wright preferred "The Biography of an American Negro." On January 22, 1944, he wrote Aswell: "I would let the reader decide if I have been courageous or not. I think the phrase 'Negro American' keeps the book related to the American scene and emphasizes the oneness of impulse, the singleness of aim of both black and white Americans." This reveals that Wright's criticism of the United States was cultural in a large sense, not merely racial.

By mid-1944 the autobiography had been set in page proofs and a jacket was ready for *American Hunger.* In the meantime, the Book-of-the-Month Club, which had been considering the work, finally accepted it as a dual selection for March 1945. It is not quite clear whether the club accepted the autobiography on

*Wright is referring here to the original two-part work.

the condition that it would include only Wright's experiences in the South, or whether Aswell himself made the suggestion. At any rate, as early as January 1944 Aswell had expressed the view that Wright should publish the first section of his autobiography separately and develop his Chicago and New York experiences into another volume. Wright seems to have agreed to do so at the time.

On August 10, 1944, Wright wrote Aswell and suggested *Black Boy* as a title for the book in its new form. Not only, he wrote, was he unable to find a better one but he considered this to be "not only a title but also a kind of heading to the whole general theme." The eight different subtitles that he also provided all articulated the Southern character of his childhood and the anxiety that had pervaded it, thus stressing the traumatic effect of the South upon black life. From Quebec, where he was vacationing at the end of August, Wright further suggested to Aswell that the review that Dorothy Canfield Fisher had written for the Book-of-the-Month Club *Bulletin* should serve as an introduction. It is clear, then, that Wright saw no objection to the publication of *Black Boy* (that is, the first part of the original autobiographical manuscript) as a separate work and that he readily complied with the request for a new conclusion that would sum up his growth in the South. Apart from that, and the deletion of a couple of paragraphs containing four-letter words, no changes were made in the original page proofs.

Extracts from the unpublished section of the autobiography appeared in the 1940s, relating Wright's early days in Chicago, his first steps as a creative writer, and his uneasy relationship with the Communist party. Brought together for the first time and, more important, put back into the organic flow of Wright's narrative, these episodes are rich with the complexity of Wright's intent. They evidence his simultaneous grappling with problems of the craft and his search for meaningful political involvement, and they vibrate with the violence of his outbursts against the frustrations of his daily life. At the same time they show Wright's attempt to invest his personal struggle with global meaning. Similar energy is apparent in Wright's unquenchable thirst for knowledge and self-expression. His setting himself to reading Gertrude Stein's *Three Lives* at the end of a nerve-racking day in the Chicago post office suggests the same intensity of commitment as his borrowing Mencken's *Prejudices* from the Memphis Public Library on a forged card. We may be tempted to smile at his somewhat naïve consideration of Proust as an example to emulate, yet we marvel at the strength of his motivation when he acknowledges:

I read Proust's *A Remembrance of Things Past*, admiring the lucid, subtle but strong prose, stupefied by its dazzling magic, awed by the vast, delicate, intricate and psychological structure of the Frenchman's epic of death and decadence. But it crushed me with hopelessness, for I wanted to write of the people in my environment with an equal thoroughness, and the burning example before my eyes made me feel that I never could. . . . If I could fasten the mind of the reader upon words so firmly that he would forget words and be conscious only of his response, I felt that I would be in sight of knowing how to write narrative.

Similar eagerness appears in Wright's desire to communicate with his fellow John Reed Club members, to militate for the cause of left-wing writing, and to be accepted in the local C.P. unit. Such frustration pervades, moreover, the narration of unsuccessful personal encounters or club meetings where progressive policies were defeated. Are we then to regret that *American Hunger* takes us far from the hopeful and potentially rosy ending of *Black Boy?* Indeed, it constitutes a more profound questioning of man's predicament in a mass consumption society whose daily practice negates its humanistic pretenses. There is no redemption for human suffering in a culture governed by the "lust for trash." Wright's impossible adjustment to the autocracy of state or party, his refusal of the mediocre prizes of so-called democracy thus assume tragic intensity. What road could he have taken in the mid 1940s? Going beyond the debunking of social myths which he attempted in "The Man Who Lived Underground," he proceeded to pose the question of the aims of civilization. His autobiography thus opens onto the Nietzschean reaches of his metaphysical novel, *The Outsider*. This endows *American Hunger* with a dimension which *Black Boy* as such never possessed, for Wright not only addresses the materialism of the South, of the United States, of Western culture; he speaks to the whole of mankind in calling for radical awareness and change. In a letter to Antonio Frasconi, a South American artist, written in November 1944, about the time he had completed *Black Boy,* Wright proclaims:

Life is sufficient unto life if it is lived and felt directly and deeply enough, and I would warn that we must beware of those who seek, in words no matter how urgent or crisis-charged, to interpose an alien and dubious curtain of reality between our eyes and the crying claims of a world which it is our lot to see only too poignantly and too briefly.

MICHEL FABRE
*Professor of American and
Afro-American Studies,
The Sorbonne*

repeatedly asked me to visit the meetings of the club, but I always
found a lame excuse to keep me from accepting.

"You'd like them and you'd agree with them," he said.

"I don't want to be organized," I said.

"Talking with them will help you in your writing," he said.

"Nobody can tell me how or what to write," I said.

"Come and meet them," he urged me. "What can you lose?"

I promised to come to a party some Saturday night, but I
did not keep my word. I felt that Communists could not possibly
have a sincere interest in Negroes. I had reached a cynical position
where I would rather have heard a white man say that he hated Negroes,
which I could have believed, than to have heard him say that he liked
Negroes, which would have made me doubt him. I did not think that
there existed whites who, through sheer strength of intellectual
effort, could lift themselves out of the culture, mores, and traditions
of their times and see the Negro objectively.

One Saturday night in autumn, sitting home with idle,
nothing to do, not caring to visit the guys I had met on my former
insurance route, not wanting to participate in a senseless bridge
game, bored with reading, and possessing only a few pennies in my
pocket, I decided to kill time by visiting the John Reed Club in
the capacity of an amused spectator. I rode to the Loop, walked
over to Michigan Avenue, found number. A dark stairway led
upwards; it did not look welcoming. What on earth of importance
could transpire in so dingy a place? I looked at the windows and
saw a faint light and vague murals along the walls.

"Well, I'll go up and take a look," I said.

Reproduced by kind permission of the Beinecke Rare Book and Manuscript Library of Yale University.

A page of the original manuscript of *American Hunger,* bearing Richard Wright's
editing. The material corresponds to page 61 in this volume.